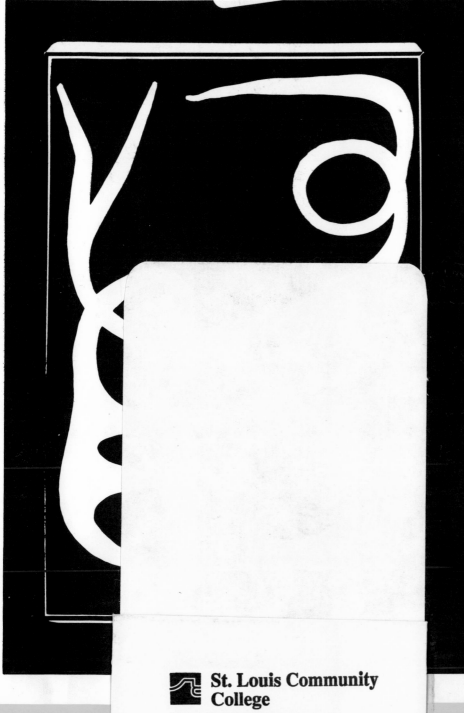

Calder

TEXT BY H. H. ARNASON

PHOTOGRAPHS BY PEDRO E. GUERRERO

Van Nostrand

Book designed by
Alexey Brodovitch

A Note on the Photographs

My primary concern, in taking the photographs for this book, has been to let Calder's works speak for themselves. I have attempted to show each individual work as it related to its environment, or if this was not possible, to show it as simply as I could; and I have tried to find for each work the most revealing attitude, and to photograph it from the point of view which best describes it.

It has been an absorbing experience to have worked so intimately with the many varied products of a single creative imagination. I am grateful to have had the opportunity to study each work, to examine the way in which it was put together, and to watch and wait for just the right moment in its movement, or find just the right camera angle. But most of all, I am grateful for the opportunity to have known the artist himself, Sandy Calder, and his wife Louisa. Their generosity in time, help and friendship has been unstinting, and my debt to them both is inexpressible.

PEDRO E. GUERRERO

New Canaan, Connecticut

In order to facilitate cross reference between the text and the works themselves, three separate indexes have been provided: the List of Illustrations, pp. x-xi, lists all the photographs in the book in the order in which they appear; the Chronology of Works, p. 186-189, lists the works alphabetically under the years of origin, and also provides details of size, medium and collection; and finally, the general Index at the end of the book furnishes both textual references and the page numbers of the illustrated works themselves.

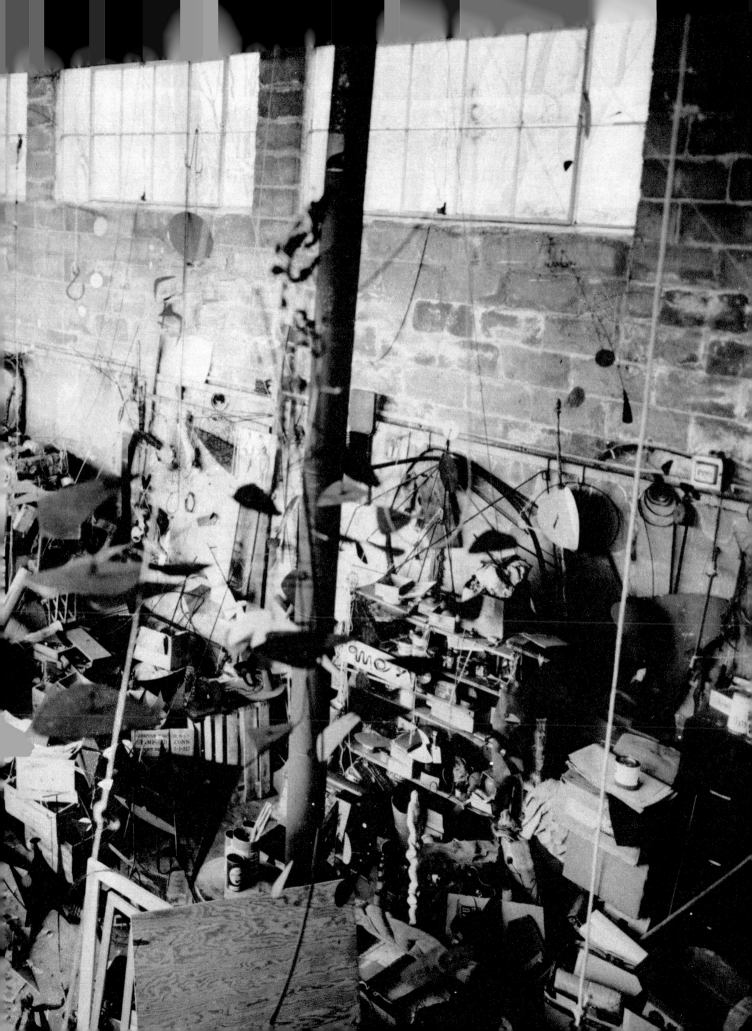

Contents

Critical Biography

Chronology

The Illustrations

Critical Biography

H. H. ARNASON

The artist and his granddaughter, Andrea Davidson

Introduction

Alexander Calder is known throughout the world as the artist who made sculpture move. He is one of the few artists in history who can lay claim to the creation of a new art form

"well-sweep" pern James Soby
`a Hartford, Conn.

which has immeasurably extended the limits and possibilities of the art of sculpture. The fact that there were isolated experiments before him in the introduction of actual physical motion into sculpture does not in any way detract from his achievement. It was Calder who first realized the full implications of the element of motion, and who explored these implications in hundreds of variations which transformed essentially technical experiments or mechanical toys into major works, involving an entire new aesthetic of sculpture.

To appreciate the achievement of Calder it is necessary to reflect on attitudes of sculptors throughout history. Sculpture, like painting

and architecture, is an art of space. Whereas architecture is traditionally defined as the art of enclosing space, and painting until the twentieth century characteristically involved the problem of creating the illusion of the third dimension or of depth on a two-dimensional surface, a work of free-standing sculpture in most of history has been thought of as a static, solid, three-dimensional object existing in and surrounded by space.

In the ancient world, the monumental sculpture of Egypt and Mesopotamia was characterized by a primary emphasis on the mass and weight of the material, most frequently stone, coupled with a rigid frontality of pose, which combined in the creation of an impression, overwhelmingly static, of forms incapable of motion, frozen into an eternal mold. Even at this stage, however, it is evident that the idea of motion was present in the sculptor's mind, although he had only a rudimentary concept of how even the illusions could be achieved. The characteristic striding pose in Egyptian figure sculpture accentuates, if anything, its essential immobility. Egyptian and Assyrian reliefs, hunting scenes or informal domestic narratives, are more successful in suggestions of movement through the groupings and interactions of personages, and more particularly of animals.

If the history of sculpture is approached through the sculptor's attitudes towards his materials—stone, clay, bronze, etc.—and the elements with which he works—space, mass, volume, line, etc.—it is possible to see a certain cyclical pattern in the great periods of sculptural achievement. Greek and Hellenistic sculpture may be said to constitute one such cycle, as do also Gothic, and Renaissance and Baroque. In terms of the broadest possible generalization it can be said that each of these three sculptural periods begins with a type of figure sculpture which is essentially static, frontalized, and with an emphasis on the solid mass of the material. In the developed phase —fifth and fourth centuries B.C., High Gothic, or High Renaissance—there is generally a greater sense of spatial existence and implied movement, achieved through some twisting of the figure in space and some interpenetration of the sculptural mass, such as the opening up of the intervals between the legs or between the arms and torso. Thus, if the *David* of Donatello or of Michelangelo (which still belongs stylistically to the Early Renaissance) is compared with Michelangelo's *Slaves,* the progression from relative frontality to a turning pose which tends to carry the eye around the figure and thus to heighten the sense of movement in three dimensions, becomes evident.

In the late phase of these stylistic cycles, the interest in spatial existence and suggested motion frequently becomes the primary for-

mal concern of the sculpture, sometimes (as in the case of Bernini's *Apollo and Daphne*) to the point where the effect begins to approximate to the pictorial rather than the sculptural. This pictorial approach characterizes much of the Rococo figure sculpture of the 18th century, which may, in fact, be considered as the last decorative phase of the Renaissance and Baroque cycle, refining and elaborating on Baroque experiments in space and motion.

Since sculpture of the 19th century is largely a series of academic, eclectic revivals of Ancient, Medieval, Renaissance, and Baroque formulae, the entire history of sculptural experiment tends to be recapitulated, although not necessarily in any logical sequence. Even Rodin, who more than any other single 19th-century sculptor made the transition from the Renaissance to the modern attitude, added little to the sculptor's formal vocabulary, except in his breaking up of surfaces to create impressionistic effects of reflected, shimmering light. This, however, was no slight achievement, emphasizing as it did the sense of organic vitality, the breathing life in the figure which in turn immensely heightened the illusion of potential movement in space.

The key word in this summary of motion experiment throughout the history of sculpture is, of course, 'illusion.' The sculptured figure never actually moved; it only seemed to move. As long as the basic instrument of

Calder-designed utensil rack at Roxbury

The house at Roxbury

The large studio, Saché, Fran

The Calders outside their Saché house

The Calder's grandson, Holton Rower, at Roxbury

sculptural expression was the human figure, any attempt to introduce actual physical movement through mechanical means would merely have resulted in some sort of toy or machine. During the 18th and 19th centuries, in fact, many such clockwork figures were produced, but these were merely amusing or mysterious gadgets which had nothing to do with the creation of sculpture. Objects powered by the wind, such as Chinese temple bells, weather vanes, or tavern signs, have also been known for centuries. An 18th-century whaling sign in which whalers' boats, mounted on a pivot, circle around the centralized whale, has been put forward as the first 'mobile.' Even this undoubtedly has antecedents; and in any event it exercised no influence on any known sculptor.

The 20th-century revolution in visual concepts of space and later of motion came first in painting through the emergence of cubism. Cubism is a logical development of impressionist and post-impressionist tendencies in late 19th-century painting, particularly as manifested in the last works of Cézanne. Picasso, joined by Georges Braque in 1907, sought to arrive at a mode of painting which would finally destroy the Renaissance concept of the painting as an imitation of the natural world, as a window opening out into naturalistic space, and would assert its own identity, its own pictorial space. By 1910 linear perspective and three-dimensional, sculptural modelling had disappeared in their paintings; color had been subordinated to a close harmony of greys, browns, and greens; and the subject (figure or still life) had been transposed into a linear geometry of intersecting and frequently transparent planes, a sort of "grid" moving within a confined depth from the frontal plane of the painting.

Cubism is the ancestor of all the abstract, geometric, classic styles in painting and sculpture of the 20th century as well as many of the abstract expressionist styles. In its later phases after 1911, its range was widened by the addition of actual objects (newspaper clippings, fragments of wallpaper, etc.) to create a new kind of reality—collage. At this stage cubist painting began to approach relief sculpture, and its significance for the creation of an entirely new concept of sculptural form became evident. This was a sculpture, at first of semi-abstract figures, then of completely abstract geometric shapes, whose technical essence was construction rather than carving or modelling. Constructed sculpture, built up of elements assimilated one to another rather than carved or modelled from an original mass, was one of the outstanding discoveries in the history of sculpture. It lent itself naturally to forms which approximated to the abstract shapes of architecture; it provided an escape from the thousands of years of slavery to the human figure as the prime and almost the only instrument of sculptural expression; and above all, it finally liberated the sculptor from the tradition that a sculpture was fundamentally a three-dimensional object surrounded by three-dimensional space. The new world of sculpture which constructivism created was perhaps best defined by Gabo and Pevsner in their 1920 Realist Manifesto:

3. We renounce volume as a pictorial and plastic form of space; one cannot measure space in volumes as one cannot measure liquid in yards: look at our space . . . what is it if not one continuous depth?

We affirm depth as the only pictorial and plastic form of space.

4. We renounce in sculpture, the mass as a sculptural element . . .
Thus we bring back to sculpture the line as a direction and in it we affirm depth as the one form of space.

5. We renounce the thousand-year-old delusion in art that held the static rhythms as the only elements of the plastic and pictorial arts.

We affirm in these arts a new element the kinetic rhythms as the basic forms of our perception of real time. . . .*

The process of construction as in architecture inevitably suggested to the sculptor the truism that the void, the depth, the space of the sculpture could be as important as or even more important than the edge, the solid, the mass. A mass or a line could frame a shaped void as effectively as, throughout history, voids had framed shaped masses. And finally, in abstract sculpture, constructed from solids and voids, lines and planes, motion need no longer merely be implied, need no longer be an optical illusion. Actual physical motion could be introduced without transforming the sculpture into a gadget or a toy.

Actual motion with its infinite implications of shifting and metamorphosed shapes would seem to be an almost inevitable and immediate consequence of constructivist sculpture. However, for some reason or other, the constructivists never seemed fully to have grasped the possibilities which lay in this direction. Gabo carried out experiments in motorized motion in the early twenties, but never proceeded with them. Abstract painting and sculpture during the twenties were explored in every conceivable direction by Mondrian, Van Doesburg, Gabo, Pevsner, and a score of others; the implications of abstract painting and sculpture for architecture were realized in the Bauhaus, and out of this environment grew the international school of modern architecture. But "every conceivable direction" still excluded actual physical motion. This was the situation when Calder reached Paris in 1926.

* *Naum Gabo.* Cambridge, Massachusetts: Harvard University Press (1957), p. 152.

I The Circus Years

Alexander Calder was born in Philadelphia on July 22, 1898. Although both his father and grandfather were distinguished sculptors and his mother a painter, he was not particularly drawn to a career of art until after he had graduated from the Stevens Institute of Technology, Hoboken, New Jersey, with a degree in Mechanical Engineering. His own inclination was towards technical and scientific pursuits and it was to these that his considerable manual dexterity tended to be devoted. After his graduation in 1919 he worked for several years at various engineering and other jobs with, however, a gradually increasing interest in drawing and painting which finally in 1923 led him to enroll as a regular student in the Art Students League of New York.

As an artist Calder was first an illustrator, a natural consequence of the environment of American art in which he grew up and in which he studied. His father had been a leading American academician in sculpture and his teachers were artists like John Sloan, George Luks, and Boardman Robinson. Drawings which he did while working as an illustrator for the *National Police Gazette* reveal principally a quick facility and considerable ability in rapid and immediate observation. The 'humorous' captions accompanying his drawings tended to the rather naive and heavy-handed vein typical of much popular American humor of the early twenties.

Calder's career as an illustrator was important to him in that it reinforced his enduring sense of the observed subject and his ability to record or suggest it with accuracy and penetration. He developed into a brilliant illustrator and caricaturist, as evidenced by several illustrated books which he produced and by the many drawings and wire sculptures in which he caught the essence of leading personalities and of personal friends.

Even more important, however is the degree to which the sense of subject penetrated and characterized his abstract constructions. It is very rare during his career that the mobiles and stabiles of Calder may be considered as purely abstract—non-objective to the point that they embody no association in nature. It is one of his distinguishing features in the world of modern art that he is an abstract sculptor whose abstractions are almost always hovering on the edge of representation. This is not to say that they assume the forms of semi-abstractions, simplified and 'modernized' figures. During his mature career he has worked characteristically in an abstract style, building his constructions from lines and planes and spaces. However, almost inevitably, somewhere along the way an association emerges—

The Circus, 1926-32, detail

a constellation, moving clouds, marine forms, a rearing horse, a fantastic monster. The association is normally recognized and captured by the artist in the title which he attaches (and which thus becomes an integral part of the finished work) to the point that it no longer can be considered simply as a relationship of abstract elements.

The sense of subject was thus established at the very beginning of the artist's career as an essential aspect of his sculpture. At that time in the early twenties, working in New York, he had little or no consciousness or understanding of modern experiments in abstract or expressionist art. Although he later formed close friendships with a few fellow artists, such as Miró and Léger, and developed a great admiration for one or two others, (notably Mondrian), Calder throughout his career has tended to isolate himself somewhat from the main currents of modern art. He has shown astonishingly little interest in the milieu of modern art, in the experiments and activities of other leading 20th-century artists—with perhaps two outstanding exceptions, Miró and Mondrian. He was in Paris for some five years, living in an environment where he was in daily contact with many of the great experimentalists, knowing many of them personally, before he emerged as an artist working in a genuinely contemporary idiom. And even then, his emergence was in the nature of a sudden conversion, the consequence of a sort of spiritual revelation.

Calder was unquestionably drawn to Paris in 1926 by the realization that there something was happening in the arts which was different from and more stimulating than anything to which he had been exposed in New York. However, in Paris, he gave no evidence of any great curiosity about the new developments. Through Stanley William Hayter, the artist-engraver, he met José de Creeft, an accomplished sculptor, but one working within relatively traditional means. His own essays in carved sculpture during the next few years broke no new ground except through the infiltration of a highly personal sense of the ludicrous. His spare time, and this seemed to be most of his time, was occupied with making toy animals and figures for his own amusement and that of his friends. These were constructed of pieces of wire, corks from wine bottles, wood and felt, and were principally characterized by the unusual verisimilitude with which a few fragments of scrap materials could be transformed into living entities capable of actions, movements, and even suggested emotional involvements, which aped humanity and the animal world with uncanny accuracy.

Throughout his life Calder has been haunted by the circus which he created in Paris during the later twenties. It was the circus which first established his fame, and it was through the circus that he first came to the attention of leading French artists and literary figures. In a sense this was a disserv-

The Circus, details

ice in that it may have delayed his emergence as a serious sculptor. Even today it is customary in many circles to think of Calder as the great humorist of modern sculpture. Certainly he is a great humorist. No one can help being delighted by the bizarre and fantastic shapes which many of his sculptures assume, the witty titles which add extra dimensions to them. Anyone who has the privilege of knowing him personally is constantly entranced by the evidences of earthy humor and biting wit of which he is capable. On the other hand, to be a humorist is not necessarily the greatest attribute which an artist may have. Whereas the creation of witty works of art is no mean achievement, and artists dedicated to wit or satire have established an enduring place for themselves, this is perhaps not the highest place. In fact, a certain dedicated humorlessness is often a characteristic of the greatest painters and sculptors. Thus it is conceivable that Calder's reputation as a humorist may have delayed and even distorted his recognition as one of the great serious artists of the 20th century.

The circus nevertheless is a fact, the principal artistic fact of Calder's life in Paris between the years 1926 and 1931. All the elements still survive and have been exhibited in the major retrospectives devoted to the

artist in recent years. As they are shown, however, they are merely an accumulation of amusing toys, into the midst of which a child would love to crawl in order that he might manipulate them. For their essence is that they are the stage properties and the actors of a living drama, in contemporary terms a happening. The circus as a fully realized work of art has been preserved for posterity in a film created in 1961 by Carlos Vilardebo. Since Calder rarely if ever attempts a performance of the circus any more, we are dependent on this film, fortunately a brilliant recapitulation, for a sense of the original character and impact of the circus as it delighted and amazed leading artists and other intellectuals of Paris in the late twenties.

When asked recently in an interview with the painter, Cleve Gray, what it was that first drew him to the circus, Calder somewhat surprised his interviewer by saying that what appealed to him was the sense of space. Since at the time that he was first attending and recording the performances in New York of the Barnum and Bailey circus Calder was essentially a clever draughtsman and facile reporter of visual events, only beginning to experiment with carved sculpture, it is possible that this emphasis on space, at least in its pictorial or sculptural sense, was in the nature of an afterthought. However, whether or not he realized its true impact at the time, in the light of his subsequent career it is not at all astonishing if his recollection is perfectly

Toy Horse and Rider, 1927

correct. The circus in its great days certainly was a tremendous experience in space—and in color and light and immensely varied and intricate movements in space—all elements which became essentials of Calder's mobiles. Thus the importance of the circus to Calder's development as an artist may conceivably have been central, but in an entirely different manner than is usually assumed.

Technically, the obvious importance of his personal circus to the artist was the constant experience he gained in the manipulation of wire, not only in the rendering of outlined faces and figures, but also in the construction of intricate, engineered apparatuses and machines, tightropes, swinging bars, cages for wild animals, bicycles and automobiles, which not only took on the illusion of reality, but also were made to function in a startlingly effective manner. Whereas he had normally drawn in rapid outline in his illustrations for the *Police Gazette*, there is no doubt that his developed style of outline figurative drawing in large degree followed and was influenced by his wire sculpture. The most accomplished circus drawings date from the early thirties, and these are almost literal transformations of wire sculpture to drawing, even to the characteristic use of the uninterrupted line.

Toy Tricycle, c. 192

Fish Pull-Toy, 1960

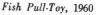

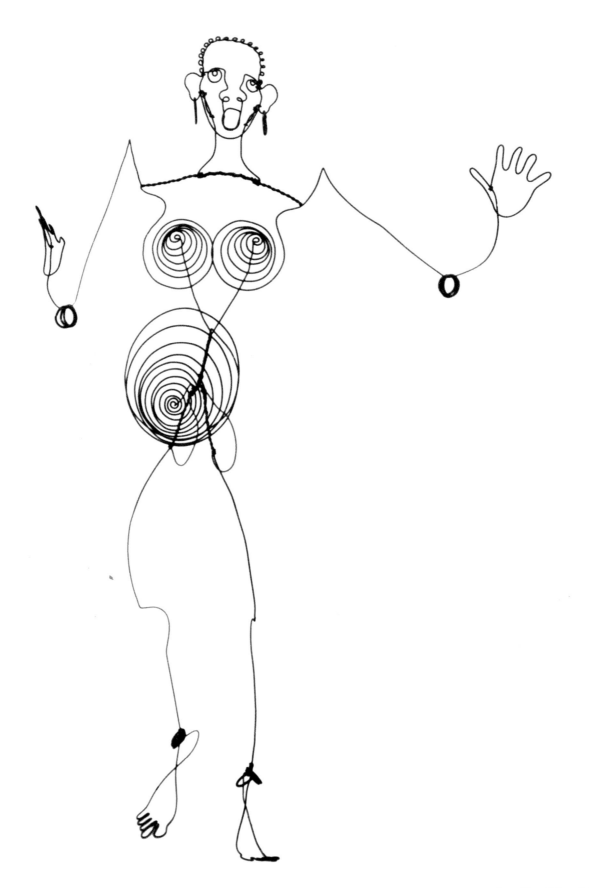

Josephine Baker I, 1926

II Figure and Portrait

The first completely realized wire sculpture is probably the *Josephine Baker I*, dated 1926. (A variant was made a few months later.) Josephine Baker, then and for many years thereafter the idol of French music halls, was a perfect subject, with her spirally undulating belly and breasts the epitome of sexual attraction, her limber legs and expressive arms suggesting the brilliant dancer and chanteuse. The figure was designed not to be placed on a base but suspended from a thread, to move and quiver in the slightest breeze; certainly a prototype of the mobile concept. Most of the first wire figure sculptures were realized in an essentially frontal, two-dimensional aspect, as though the artist was not yet aware of the fundamental departure he was making in the art of sculpture. For these figures presented, in the most modest and easy manner, an entire repertoire of scuptural space/mass reversals in which lines were used to outline the voids or spaces which took the place of the solid masses of which the figure was constituted.

At this point Calder was not acquainted with Gabo and Pevsner's *Realist Manifesto* and certainly was completely unaware that he was beginning to put this manifesto into practical effect. He was probably not even too much aware of the fact that he was creating sculpture, much less sculpture which was on

the verge of one of the great innovations in the history of the art.

The wire sculpture of the next few years demonstrated a continually growing consciousness of the sculptural implications and possibilities of the particular form which he had embarked upon simply as a sort of personal divertissement. A *Horse* of 1927, while still rendered as an essentially static, profile view, had doubled lines in the body which increased the sense of volume; and a sign for his wire sculpture exhibition of 1928 at the Weyhe Gallery included an acrobat figure hanging by his knees and holding the actual sign. The figure was suspended from a single hook so that it swayed and turned in space. While the origin of the mobile has variously been traced to Chinese wind bells, Victorian glass parlor ornaments, 18th-century animated toys, or even swing hammocks, this exhibition sign draws one of the closest analogies to the swinging signs which for centuries ornamented the façades of taverns and vendors of foods.

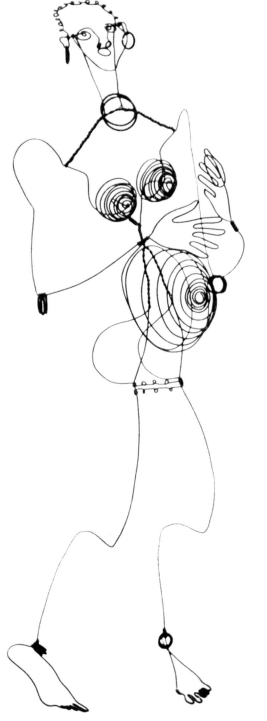

Josephine Baker II, 1926

During the first years in Paris (with frequent returns to the United States) Calder continued to develop his own carved sculpture in a direction curiously at odds with the wire sculpture or even the circus toys. Animals such as the *Cow* of 1928 revealed his wonderful eye for what might be called the significant pose or movement, instantaneously caught to achieve all the shock of immediate recognition and rendered with a delightful and sympathetic humor. This particular work also suggests the artist's early and continuing fascination with the found object, in this case a gnarled piece of wood which probably evoked immediately the image of the cow slowly and patiently turning her head to observe, with a thoroughly bovine glance, whatever is disturbing her.

The most impressive carved animal is unquestionably the *Horse*, 1928, in the Museum of Modern Art, New York, which is some 30 inches long. This not only has a most appealing quality of lumbering equine stupidity, but also might be classified as one of the earlier examples of constructed sculpture by the artist, since it is formed of three parts with fore and aft legs neatly mortised into the torso. The early carved animals of Calder undoubtedly owe something to de Creeft, but in their affectionate humor and simplified but highly recognizable forms they remind one most immediately of the animal carvings of the first great 20th-century American carver, John Flannagan.

Certain attempts at simplified, carved wood figure compositions, e.g. *Three Men High*, 1928, are reminiscent of works by de Creeft or of the American sculptor, Chaim Gross. In this instance the figures are carved with a geometric blockiness which suggests that Calder may have also been looking at some of the cubist sculptures of Lipchitz, without making a real attempt at emulation.

When one turns from this rather routine attempt at slightly abstracted carving back to similar circus subjects done with incredible economy in twisted and shaped wires, the entire performance suddenly springs into life. The wire *Acrobats*, dated 1929, is a tour de force of expressive action realized with only a few twists of the wire. The supporting acrobat stumbles and totters as he strives to keep his balance, blinded by his partner's hand which has slipped down over his eyes, while the partner frantically fights to maintain his one-hand stand. Rarely in the history of sculpture, or of circus acrobatics, has a total collapse been so imminent.

On the other hand, *The Brass Family*, 1929, is a marvel of poise and control. The gigantic anchor man supports his numerous family with an ease that is almost contemptuous, and each member of the family does his or her stint with bored proficiency, utterly confident in the security of his underpinning and his own ability to assume his rightful place in the human pyramid. In these wire sculptures and the related drawings of this period it is

Horse, 1928, Collection The Museum of Modern Art, New York. Acquired through the Lillie P. Bliss Bequest.

Cow, 1928

Horse, 1927

Hercules and Lion, 1929

Helen Wills, 1928

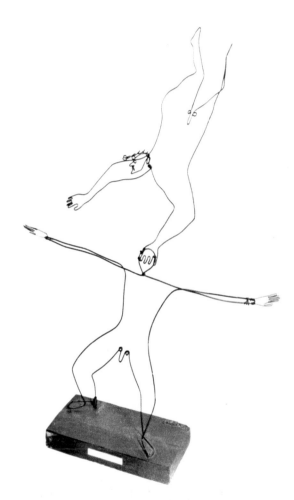

Acrobats, 1928

Three Men High, 1928

The Brass Family, 1929

necessary to emphasize the illustrative, humorous or satirical aspects, since these are the elements which are still dominant in the artist's approach. *The Brass Family*, although now on a large scale, 64 inches high, is still essentially a flat, outline drawing translated into wire. The group is completely frontalized and, despite some suggestion of linear internal modelling, has the effect of a two-dimensional drawing on a two-dimensional surface. This is equally true of the even larger *Spring*, 1929, which is in essence a figure, 95 inches high, drawn in wire as though with a single, continuous line. Only the signature, descriptively shaped, departs from the attenuated linear simplification of the figure.

The bawdy humor which is suggested in this work recurs again in the even more monumental (if the term can be properly applied to sculpture which consists entirely of space) *Romulus and Remus*, 1928, perhaps the most important of all the early wire figure sculptures. The she-wolf is a good 112 inches long and every inch the picture of contented maternity. Romulus and Remus scamper after her dugs like good infant wolves (the dugs, like the appropriate members of the boys themselves, formed simply but with graphic perfection from a series of wooden door stops, whose possibilities must at once have caught the artist's eye). Works like this are wonderful instances of Calder's inventiveness as well as his incredible proficiency in suggesting personal characteristics and complex relation-

ships with a simple twist of wire. The cavalier manner in which the artist treats his own works is evidenced by the fact that when they were sought out for the retrospective at the Guggenheim Museum, they were found rolled up into balls of wire which he was compelled painstakingly to unravel and reshape. This casual attitude, arising from Calder's fantastic productivity, is nevertheless somewhat deceptive. In fact, he seems to have almost total recall concerning not only every piece he ever created, but all the circumstances, including the present location.

Considered as a traditional sculptural organization of three-dimensional space, one of the most effective of these wire sculptures is *Hercules and the Lion*, 1929. Again with the simplest possible means, Hercules is shown in a space-twisting contraposto, flexing his mighty muscles while in the process of tearing the unfortunate lion's head off. However, it is probable that the pose of the group was suggested by the traditional Renaissance representations, and that the use of the spiral composition to render spatial existence was a result of these models rather than any sudden awakening of the artist to the spatial possibilities of his medium.

26

This is not to assume that Calder was at that time completely indifferent to the problems of space in sculpture or in drawing. His training in painting and sculpture had been largely within a somewhat progressive realistic tradition, which was still rooted in Renaissance attitudes towards linear and atmospheric perspective in painting and contraposto in sculpture as means of creating illusions of depth or three-dimensional existence. It is only that while modelling in space through the media of outline drawing and of wire, he was not as yet fully aware of the entire new world of space which was literally at his finger tips.

It is probably in the drawings of these years (1926-1932) that the growing consciousness of space organization becomes most evident. The circus drawings of 1931 and 1932 are marvels of economy and of linear spacing on the page. *Balancing Lady*, 1931, is established in frightening solitude within vast empty space, defined by the single line of the tightrope disappearing diagonally back into depth.

The Tumblers, 1931, float effortlessly through empty space in a manner curiously reminiscent of hunting scenes in prehistoric cave paintings. Sometimes the emptiness is given a specific locale, as in exotic scenes like *Couple*

in Egypt, 1931, where the vastness is that of the desert, defined by outlined pyramids on the horizon. Even the frenzied crowd of *Ben Hur*, 1931, is concentrated on the central buttress of the hippodrome within the large spaces of the race course, isolated, but in no sense as completely as the absorbed street cleaner bending to his task and happily oblivious of what is coming around the corner.

From the very beginning of his career, Calder had particularly relished the making of portrait drawings and caricature heads of his friends and of notables of the day. These translated easily into wire drawings of individuals which if anything, are even more striking thirty years later in the impact with which they recall personalities of the late twenties and thirties. Calvin Coolidge, Helen Wills, Jimmy Durante, Fernand Léger, as well as Josephine Baker, are given a new life to all who remember them as they were then; and intimate portraits such as that of his wife, *Louisa*, carry an affectionate resemblance which persists to the present day. Léger, a good friend, appears as an impressively hatted, forceful, large-nosed, moustached individual, seemingly sure of himself but with a somewhat wary glance.

Unraveling *Spring* and *Rom*
and Remus, in 1

Spring, 1929

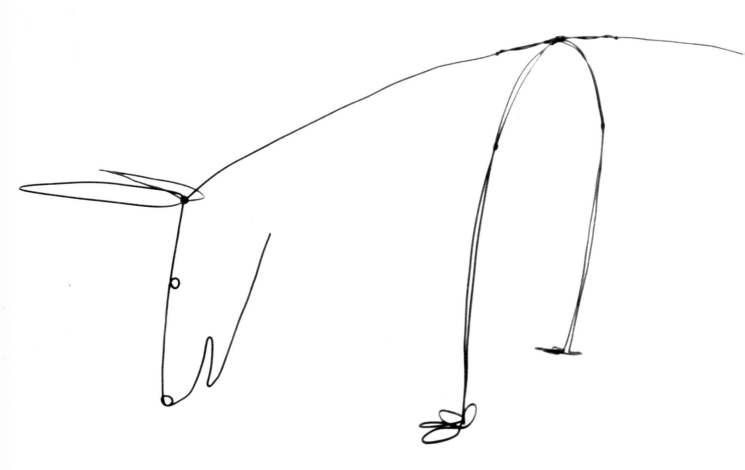

Romulus and Remus, 1928

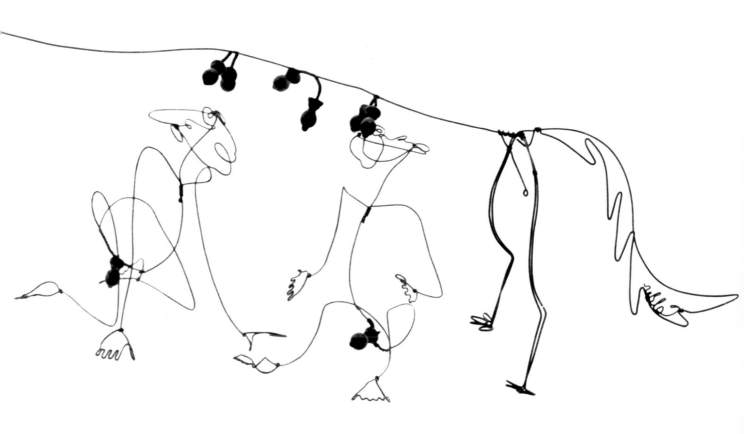

Balancing Lady, 1931

Couple in Egypt, 1931

Dancer with Flutist, 1931

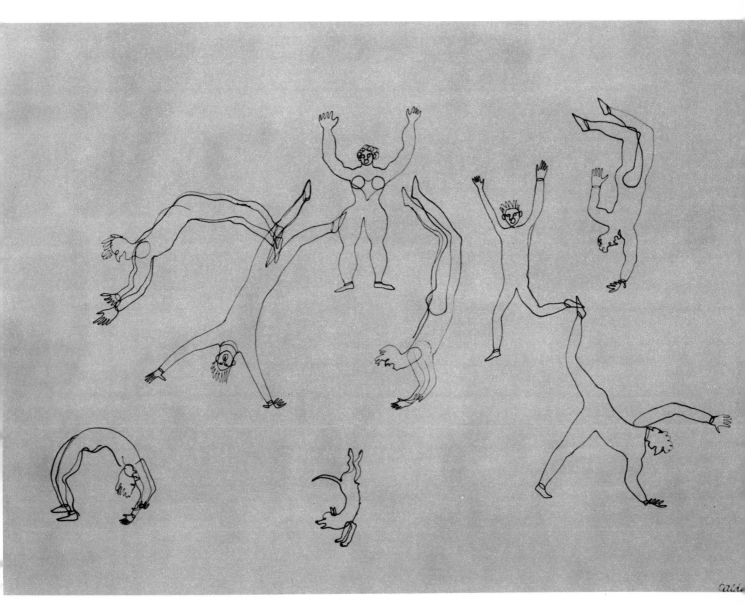

The Tumblers, no. II, 1931

Varese, 1931

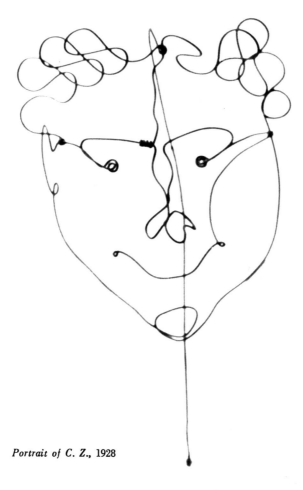

Portrait of C. Z., 1928

Louisa, 1931

Composition, 1930

III   Abstraction and the Birth of the Mobile

During 1929 Calder exhibited his wire figure sculptures and portraits in New York, Berlin, and Paris, and again gave performances of his circus when he returned to Paris in the spring of 1930. Many notables continued to attend the performances, the most significant, in terms of his effect on Calder's subsequent work, being Piet Mondrian. Despite his normal diffidence Calder was sufficiently impressed by his friend William Einstein's account of Mondrian's importance that he in turn paid a visit to the latter's studio. Mondrian's studio in Paris and later in New York was an extension of his painting transformed into a total, three-dimensional environment.

It was a reflection of his lifelong desire to make of easel painting something more total, not something to be hung on a wall and observed from the outside, but a space which could be entered by the spectator and which would surround him completely and absorb him into its totality. Something like this must have happened to Calder on the occasion of his visit. He was unquestionably at a point of his development when he felt a passionate need for a new direction, when all his seemingly haphazard experiments were reaching some sort of climax which only needed a violent catalyst to bring it into sharp focus. He has recorded the experience in Mondrian's

studio, the stark white walls accented in areas of red and blue and yellow, the placing of every object so that it became part of a complete, rectangular, static harmony. "I thought at the time how fine it would be if everything there moved, though Mondrian himself did not approve of this idea at all. I went home and tried to paint. But wire, or something to twist or tear or bend, is an easier medium for me to think in." (*The Painter's Object*, edited by Myfanwy Evans, London, 1937, quoted in Sweeney, *Calder*, p. 26.)

The paintings produced during this brief digression (*Composition*, 1930) are important documents as the artist's first efforts at completely abstract statement. However, it is unlikely that they added a great deal to the history of abstract art. On the other hand, the abstract wire constructions produced under the inspiration of Mondrian during the latter part of 1930 and 1931 marked the most significant single breakthrough in the artist's entire career, in a way more drastic than the next move into motion. The importance lay in the abandonment of representation and the emergence of an approach more completely abstract than anything he has done before or since. From Mondrian, Calder took the use of strong primary colors—reds, blues, yellows, blacks and whites—which he has continued to

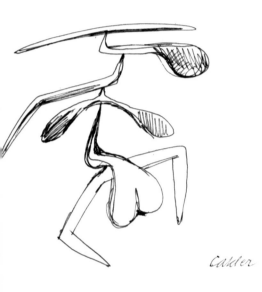

Calder

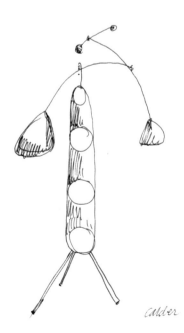

Calder

use in his sculpture. However, in the first exhibition in the Percier Gallery (Paris, April, 1931) of static wire sculptures—"stabiles" as Jean Arp named them on the occasion of the first exhibition of mobiles, a year later—he studiously avoided the rectangle, and composed his abstractions of wire circles, wire rods extending into space, small wooden balls, and some shaped metal plaques.

He reluctantly included some of his wire portraits at the insistence of the gallery director, and a comparison of these with the new abstractions is illuminating. What becomes apparent is that even if Calder had not given a great deal of thought to the implications of his wire portraits as space-defining linear outlines, through them his awareness of space as the central concomitant of his constructions was continually developing. The portrait heads, generally hung at the top of the wall above the abstractions (which were arranged on benches along the walls) seem to have a definite relationship, to the point where the abstractions take on the character of space volumes deriving from the portrait heads.

Whether this relationship is real or imagined, or whether Calder was more aware of some of the constructivist experiments of Gabo and Pevsner than is generally realized, there is no question that in the Percier exhibition he emerged at a single stroke from the cocoon of brilliant illustrator and delightful humorist to the full flight of sculptor-in-space. It is apparent that, when he attempted to define in his own terms what the revelation in Mondrian's studio meant to him—to find the solution to "putting Mondrian into motion" after a few frustrating attempts at Mondrian-inspired paintings—he realized that the problem of the abstract sculptor was entirely different from that of the abstract painter. And the problem was not actually so difficult for him. For years he had been playing with space volumes in wire sculpture. All he needed to do was to eliminate the representational element, the association, and to concentrate on the definition of the volumes with the simplest possible means. The most obvious means was the wire circle—sometimes defined by a second perimeter, sometimes by a line or angle moving out into space, sometimes by the accent of a disk or a ball beginning or terminating the line.

Curiously enough, the device of motion in sculpture seems to have developed almost in a distinct and separate pattern in Calder's sculpture. In the circus he had continually been involved in the creation of motion and action and balance. The acrobats, released by a spring, leaped from bar to bar. The tightrope walker balanced with precarious ease. The exotic dancer undulated with lascivious energy. The stretcher bearers came galloping in to rescue the knife-thrower's lady, impaled by his ineptitude. However, all of this was essentially the play of toys, without apparent serious significance for sculpture. In 1928, on the occasion of his exhibition in New York at

39

Model for World's Fair '39, 1938

Dancing Torpedo Shape, 1932

The White Frame, 1934

the Fifty-sixth Street Gallery, he made a wire frame simulating a goldfish bowl through which the fish swam, motivated by a hand crank. This may have been inspired by an exhibition of 18th-century mechanical birds in cages, which were on view in an adjoining gallery. It led to a number of other experiments in mechanized mobiles during the next year or two, some of which were powered by small electric motors and involved purely abstract elements of springs and disks. *Motorized Mobile*, c. 1932 (Hirshhorn Collection) already represents a highly sophisticated approach to the problem of abstract design in motion. The wire sculptures in the exhibition at the Percier Gallery in 1931 were not intended to move except as a delicate tendril of wire might vibrate in a current of air. However, the wedding of these stabiles to the motion machines was such an obvious next step that the artist was proceeding with it even before the Percier exhibition had opened.

The first group of motorized mobiles was shown in 1932 at the Galerie Vignon in Paris. These included a number of constructions (*The Arc and the Quadrum*, 1932, Berkshire Museum, Massachusetts) which simply translated stabiles of the preceding year into motion. In this work the motor creates a subtle vibrating relationship between the red ball suspended on the end of a fine wire, and the heavier wire hook which seems to be attempting to swallow it. The motion is only slightly more complicated than the vibrating rod en-

titled *Kinetic Sculpture* with which Gabo, in 1920, introduced actual motion into modern abstract sculpture. But Calder the engineer, with years of experiment behind him in making his circus toys move, progressed immediately far beyond such an elementary first step.

The *Dancing Torpedo Shape*, 1932, still motorized, by playing different shapes in motion against one another begins to set up complex mathematical relationships of movement in space. *A Universe*, 1934, is also an adaptation to motion (similar to others he had made as early as 1932) of a stabile *Universe*, 1931, in the Percier exhibition. In both cases the frame consists of two circles, one vertical and the other horizontal, intersecting at right angles. These are bisected by a heavy wire line shaped in an S, or double curve. In the stabile, two balls are suspended on the end of two thin wires moving out into space at the top. In the mobile the two balls are set within the vertical circle. One is on a long diagonal wire joining the upper part of this circle to a rod inserted in the base; the other is fixed on a second S-curve wire, attached at the top to the first, heavier one, and at the bottom to a groove in the base. The motor rotates the balls on their wires at different rates of speed, making them move back and forth within the circular frame. The motion is again a complex series of predictable relationships, worked out to a large but finite number of combinations.

The difficulty with the motorized mobile, which Calder soon recognized, was that it inevitably involved these predictable mathematical relationships. For an artist whose passionate interests lay in man and nature, in living, organic patterns rather than geometric ones, pure abstraction based on geometry very soon began to become a strait jacket. Even in his first exhibition of stabiles, as noted, the abstractions maintained reminiscences of the portrait heads; lines and color shapes, and sometimes entire separate constructions, frequently seemed to interact with one another in attitudes suggesting human or animal reactions—of menace or curiosity or affection.

Fait tableau du "Banquet des Pompiers" a New York, en honeur de Brancusi, sans savoir qui était Brancusi

The artist's need for some sort of association in nature is apparent in the titles which he felt compelled to attach. Wire circles with satellite wooden balls obviously became *Universes*. The first motorized mobiles, even when they involved abstract shapes, interacted in an even more positive sense. The shapes

lunged at each other or climbed over one another in a slightly mad, dada fashion which had none of the precision of the normal machine, but brought to mind how a Duchamp ready-made or a Rube Goldberg machine drawing might have acted if actually set into motion.

Despite the highly personal nature of the motorized mobiles, there was no way in which they could be made to avoid the element of the predictable. In order to operate, they must have some mathematical base—the movements at some point inevitably must repeat themselves. What was missing was that element of chance—the intuitive or spontaneous, as contrasted with the rational or calculated—which to Calder has always been, whether he defined it or not, the essence of a work of art.

Over the years the artist has continued from time to time to play with motorized mobiles. As late as 1962 he produced his most monumental version in the *Four Elements* in Stockholm which is some 30 feet high. However, already by 1932 he had begun to explore the possibilities of mobiles powered only by currents of air, and in these he discovered the medium by which he will always be remembered.

A Universe, 1934, Collection The Museum of Modern Art, New York.

Universe, 1931

Mobile, c. 1934

IV   Mobiles of the Thirties

The Percier exhibition inevitably drew Calder more closely into the orbit of the leading abstract artists then in Paris, artists like Jean Arp, Theo van Doesberg and Jean Hélion, as well as Mondrian. He was now recognized as a serious artist with a highly significant personal statement, and perhaps he, himself, suddenly became aware of this fact. Despite the fact that he has never had much interest in art movements or artists organizations, he was induced to join *Abstraction-Création*, the association which at that time was attempting to bring together the various wings of pure abstract art which had germinated earlier in Russia, Holland, Germany and France.

The most important single relationship of his life with another artist grew during these years in Paris. This was his friendship with Joan Miró. Miró had visited a circus performance in 1928 and Calder had repaid the visit by dropping in at Miró's studio. Although the few examples of Miró's works which were then in the studio made no particular impression on Calder at the time, gradually over the next few years he not only began to admire the Spaniard's painting greatly, but also to realize that his own basic sympathies lay in the direction of Miró's abstract surrealism based on organic forms, rather than in the direction of Mondrian's pure plastic geometry. What

appealed to Calder was obviously that Miró's forms, no matter how far removed from representation, always suggested their origin in nature and always included the elements of life and organic interaction. They were realistic in terms of their own private reality. This was basically what he wanted in his own sculpture.

Thus in 1932, shortly after the Galerie Vignon exhibition of mechanical mobiles, he began to produce his wind-powered mobiles. One of the first of these was a standing mobile entitled *Calderberry Bush*, 1932—a long rod, leaning diagonally, supported from a small loop at the apex of a wire pyramid. To the base of the rod was attached a heavy ball which acted as a counterweight for the upper elements, a frame of horizontal wires extending at right angles from a vertical wire with a small ball at the top and a somewhat larger one at the bottom. At the ends of the parallel horizontal wires are a series of graduated disks. The entire structure is in a delicate state of balance, and may be set into a graceful pattern of interlocking movements by the slightest breath of air or thrust of the hand. This very early standing mobile follows the forms of the 1931 stabiles in its geometric components, and is already as sophisticated in both its design and its engineering as any-

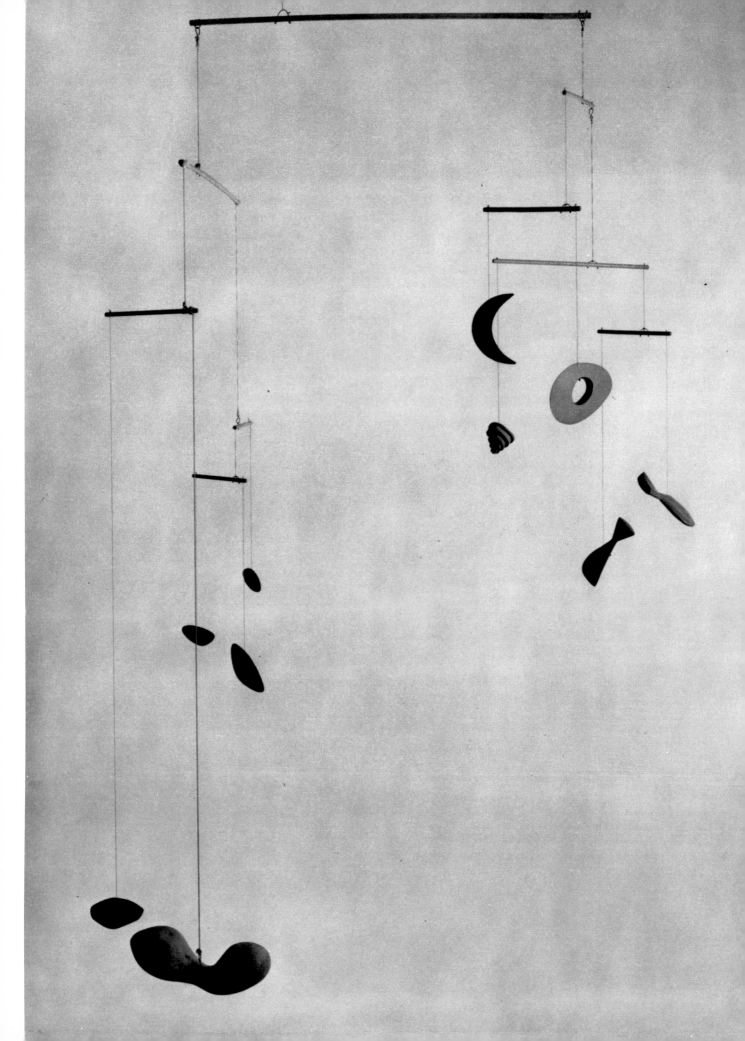

thing he was to produce over the next twenty years. As a matter of fact, it embodied forms and elements to which he was to return on several occasions, most recently in certain works of the sixties.

The characteristic hanging mobiles of the thirties were generally more simple and rudimentary than *Calderberry Bush*, frequently embodying the artist's growing interest in found objects, particularly those which contained qualities of color and texture. A series of hanging mobiles dated 1934 to 1936 illustrate this early or 'archaic' stage in Calder's career. These involve relatively simple patterns of balance with light wooden horizontal rods, from which are suspended by strings various objects such as fragments of broken colored glass, pottery shards, buttons, and even occasionally a spoon or some other utensil which happened to be available and to give the needed balance. These 'poor man's mobiles' (no longer, alas!) composed of the cheapest kinds of materials, nevertheless achieve the greatest elegance through the delicacy of their balance and the richness of light reflections which the colored glass fragments emit.

Occasionally the found objects are accompanied by thin strips of metal cut by the artist into free forms which suggest the organic shapes in Miró's paintings, and gradually these deliberately formed shapes begin to supersede the found objects. *Mobile*, c. 1934, is one of the earliest of the hanging mobiles in which the suspended elements are all organic shapes—three balanced units, one large one balancing two smaller ones, each consisting of two free-form varicolored plaques intersecting at right angles. Despite its simplicity and the use of the most inexpensive and transitory materials, this work embodies many of the elements of the most elaborate and monumental later mobiles. Although merely entitled *"Mobile"*—as was Calder's habit in most of these early works—the shaped disks here begin to suggest natural formations, clouds or birds or butterflies, hovering near or drifting past one another. It is another evidence of the recurring sense of subject to which the artist always returns.

In fact, the wind mobiles of the thirties might be classified in terms of the artist's gradual return from his excursion into pure geometry back to an art of subject association.

In another sense it was never actually a return, since literal representation had now been abandoned to be resumed only for occasional pieces in lighter vein. The progress was forward rather, to the discovery of another, new kind of subject—one in which essentially abstract constructions could be given an extra dimension by suggested associations which the imagination of the spectator could enlarge upon in accordance with his sensitivity.

The transition from geometric abstraction to a personal form of abstract expression, based on the complex interaction of organic shapes, was not a simple or direct progression. Despite the ultimate predominance of the latter tendency, geometry has never been totally abandoned. Periodically, constructions, mobiles or stabiles are produced of a geometric purity approximating to the first stabiles. Even these, however, now invariably have the stronger sense of subject which marks all the mature works. A hanging mobile of c. 1935 consists of only some different-colored, different-sized wooden balls arranged in precise balance. Certain standing mobiles of the same date return to the circle as a frame for a few chaste hanging objects. Other mobiles such as *The Black Clouds,* 1936, balance a number of graduated circular disks against two or three large, elongated free forms. This work is another evidence that pure formal relations soon ceased to be enough for Calder.

By 1936 the neutral designation of *"Mobile"* had already begun to pall and descriptive names were introduced, to add once more the dimension of association. It is possible that the artist found himself in the same dilemma as many of the American abstract expressionists in the fifties. In their determination to emphasize the non-subject nature of their paintings, these artists had used numbers or letter symbols to identify them. However, almost without exception they found that it is extremely difficult to recall the specific work on the basis of the code number, and as a result they reverted to some sort of descriptive title. In Calder's case, the re-emergence of titles was much more the consequence of the fact that some sort of subject, no matter how *récherché,* bizarre or outrageous, was essential to him.

By 1938 the hanging mobiles, which still constituted the bulk of his production, had become increasingly complicated and sophisticated. In *Three Antennae,* 1938, he uses a wide variety of cut shapes of metal, loosely triangular, semicircular, crescent, or ovoid with centers cut out to increase the spatial suggestion. Here the hanging frames are no longer simply balanced rectangles, but he introduces long looping wires which seem physically to embrace the void which they define. As the suspended metal shapes and the cord or wire frames which hold them are var-

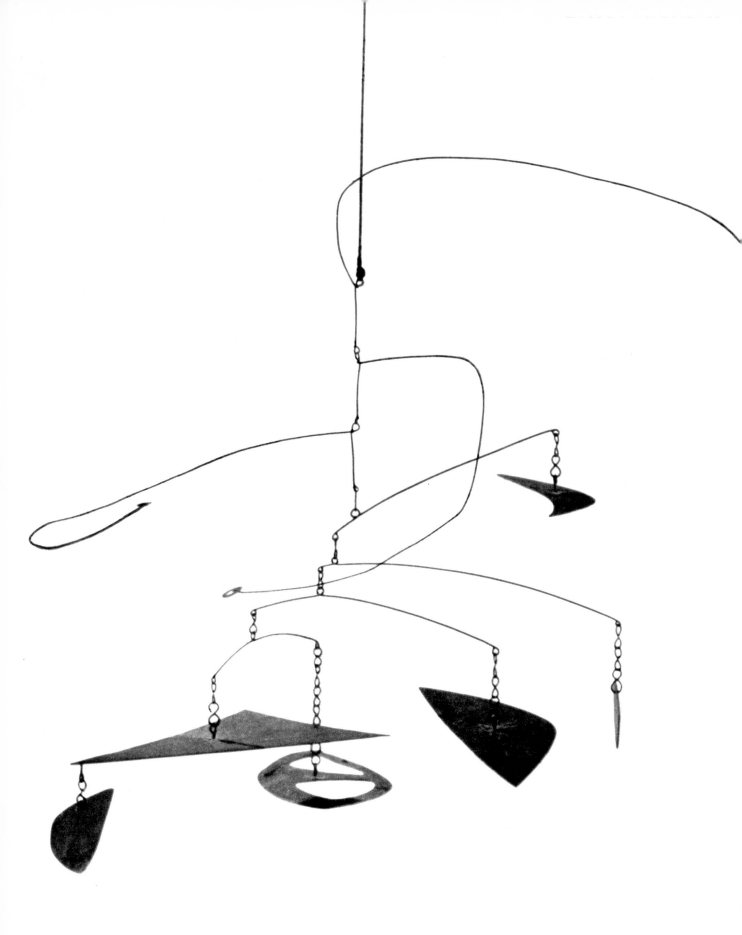

Three Antennae, 1936

ied and complicated, so are the spatial gyrations of which the mobiles are capable. The earlier ones, of glass fragments hanging at different intervals but more or less on a single plane, normally achieved a gentle form of total rotation. Mobiles such as the *Black Clouds* or *Three Antennae* now can be made to loop and swirl up and down as well as round or back and forth. And with these the artist was only beginning to explore the possibilities of movement in space. His technical knowledge was enlarging daily, as was his imaginative appreciation of the infinite pos-

sibilities of the medium which he had discovered. From this point forward, variations, elaborations, and expansions of the mobile concept have poured forth in a flood which is only limited by the physical energy which could be expended in a day's work. And even this seems unlimited.

The character of the wind mobile is a subtle variation of movement which is at most comparable to the swift but gentle flow of clouds on a windy day. The concept of the mobile—sculpture in motion—has fascinated a number of photographers, who have tried to capture its essence in photographic essays, particularly through the medium of multiple flash. Most successful was undoubtedly Calder's friend, Herbert Matter, in his motion picture on the artist. Even here Calder was not entirely happy about all the analogies in nature—drifting clouds, waves upon the beach, wind in the leaves of trees. While these are unquestionably legitimate analogies in terms of subject association, it is always dangerous to push an analogy too far. Far more distorting to the artist's intentions and the actual visual effects of his mobiles are the various stroboscopic photographs that have been made, which have the effect of putting the mobiles into orbit at the speed of sound. These make beautiful photographs, but they have little to do with the actual effect of the artist's works.

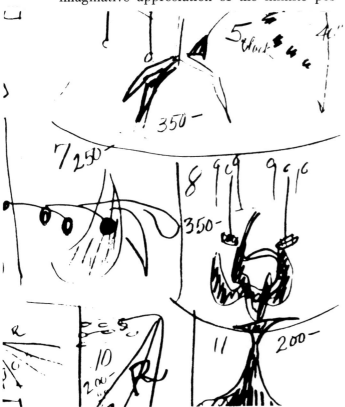

Constellation with Quadrilateral, 1943

V   Experiments in Wood

During the thirties Calder continued from time to time to produce static sculptures, 'stabiles,' which were frequently simply his old wood carvings under an elegant new name. To call them the 'old' wood carvings is not quite fair or accurate, since they demonstrated a progressive experiment at least comparable to the mobiles. The principal interest which the wood or wood and metal sculptures illustrated was the exploration of the found object, sometimes to delightful and fascinating effect. An essential aspect of Calder's imagination is its ability to see in the most commonplace object, a stone or a twig, the image of some fantastic or ludicrous monster. On the occasion of a visit to the present writer's office his eye was caught by a small paper weight of brass, shaped like a pebble. Idly he picked up a marking pencil, and with half a dozen lines had transformed it into a somewhat sinister frog. Something in the pebble-shaped brass had suggested "frog," and it took only a moment to transform the image into reality.

Shark and Whale, c. 1933 consists merely of two elements, a tusk-shaped vertical wooden block, roughly scored, resting on the flat root end, and a loosely and roughly shaped crescent, balanced on the point. Whether the tusk shape is the shark lunging up at the whale or whether the curved piece of wood is the shark circling around the tusk-shaped whale is probably immaterial. The artist was obviously intrigued by a balanced relationship of the two pieces of wood which he worked only slightly to accentuate whatever image they suggested. With the addition of the title the imagination of the spectator was left free to develop any personal images that might come to mind.

Gibraltar, 1936, is perhaps a more obvious image, the block of wood roughly hacked into a kind of Gibraltar-like pyramid. The oval-shaped disk with one flattened end, which encircles the pyramid and which itself supports a white ball and two vertical wires, one surmounted by a smaller colored ball and the other by a crescent shape, may suggest a frame of celestial bodies or something as mundane as air traffic. The exact interpretation is probably of no significance and perhaps could not even be defined by the artist. A group of shapes, massive or linear, materials of wood and metal, were worked into a sculpture, carved and constructed. What emerged suggested the rock of Gibraltar, and Gibraltar it became. This sculpture has a particular interest in that it attempts to assimilate different aspects of Calder's sculptural explorations, specifically those of wood carving and of

Constellation, 1943

Constellation c. 1943

Shark and Whale, c. 1933

geometric construction. The experiment was pursued in a radically different form during 1943 and 1944 when wartime shortages of metals led him to return to serious carving in a series of abstract *Constellations.*

Aside from these, which are of considerable importance, Calder's carvings from the late thirties forward seem to have taken on the nature of an avocation, something done for his own relaxation and amusement, or the entertainment first of his children and later of his grandchildren. In the same way and for the same reasons he has continued to make toys and gadgets of all descriptions as well as delightful naturalistic objects, such as suspended fish made from gaily colored glass fragments. In fact, the Calders' homes at Roxbury, Connecticut and Saché, France, are

filled to overflowing with such useful gadgets and decorative objects which have been produced over the years by the artist's unlimited imagination and energy.

The later carvings sometimes emphasize the found object—as in the case of *Apple Monster,* 1938, in which a gnarled branch picked up in his orchard is transformed, with the absolute minimum of adjustment, into a most convincing fantastic beast. After this date it is rare to find a carving involving even this degree of representation, although in *Wooden Bottle with Hairs,* 1943, Calder takes an abstract, organic shape, resembling at some remove a bottle, and by attaching a cluster of pointed objects to it with wire he creates an image highly suggestive of some particularly repellent form of animal life.

Apple Monster, 1938

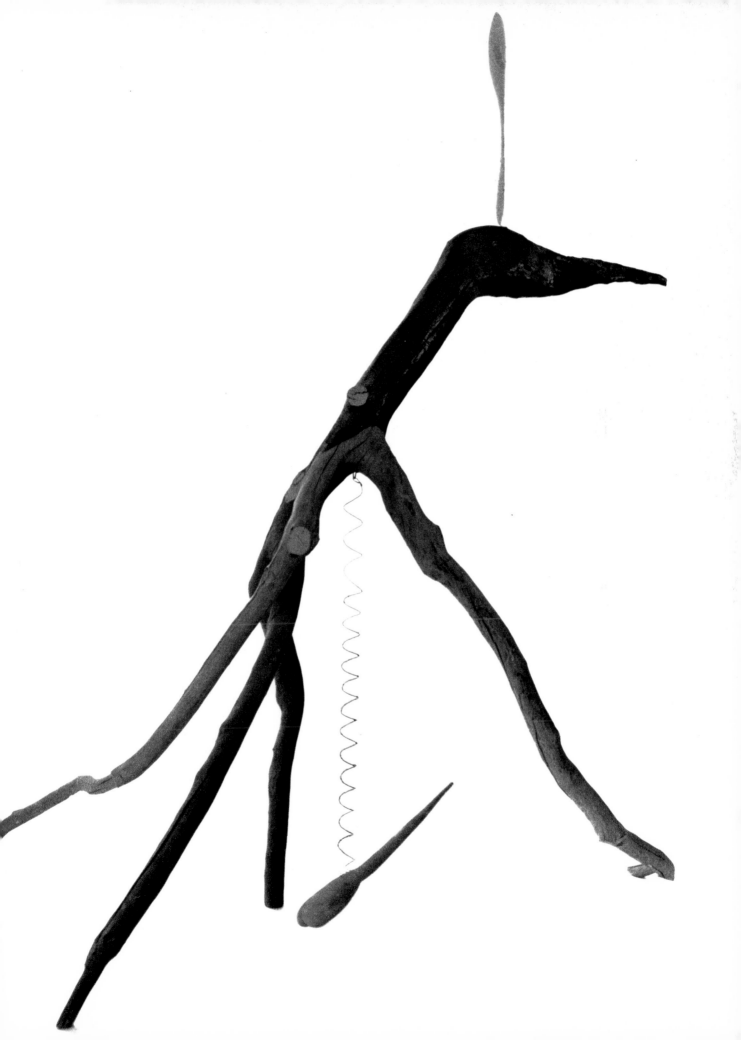

Wooden Bottle with Hairs, 1943

Gibraltar, 1936

VI Major Motor Mobiles

Periodically Calder has returned to the motorized mobile, and one of his most monumental works, created in 1962, involves motor power. This is the *Four Elements* in Stockholm. However, this is actually the realization of a project which was first explored as early as 1936; in fact there are very few new experiments in automation after 1940. *The White Frame*, 1934, is the largest as well as the second-earliest of a type which might be referred to as a 'motorized relief.' Set against a plain, flat background are a few elements, a spiral wire in the left corner, a large suspended disk towards the right side, and between them, also suspended on wires, a white ring and two small balls, one red and one black. Put into motion, the large disk swings back and forth as a pendulum, the spiral rotates rapidly to create a multiple spiral effect, and the ring and balls spin.

A somewhat comparable work is *Quattro Pendulati*, 1943, in which however, as the title suggests, the motion is simplified to four painted pendulums set against a board panel. A different approach to the motorized mobile is to be seen in *The Orange Panel*, 1943, in which a group of amoeba-like shapes, orange-red, black and white, are suspended against an orange panel and are so wired together that they achieve a curious interplay, suggestive of the assimilation and separation of micro-organisms seen under the microscope. It is perhaps significant that these latter experiments in motorized mobiles were made during World War II at a time when metal for the wind mobiles and stabiles had become scarce. *The Orange Panel*, its shapes suggesting both the influence of Miró and more specifically that of Jean Arp, represented an important departure from the mechanical monotony inherent in most of the previous motorized mobiles towards a freer, more spontaneous and varied organic motion which had great potentials for development. The principles have, in fact, been pursued by other younger kinetic sculptors, who have followed in Calder's path, more than by Calder himself.

The most ambitious of Calder's motorized mobiles, as stated, is the *Four Elements*, created in 1962 for the Moderna Museet in Stockholm. This is based on an original idea developed in 1936 in a small mobile entitled *Dancers and Sphere*, a free-standing work consisting of two colored metal upright elements, suggestive of figures with curving, outstretched arms. Between them is a diagonal, torpedo shape, and above them a ball attached to the base by two wires which form two arms of a triangle. The whole is powered by a group of small turntables, and when these are set in motion, the figures whirl, the tor-

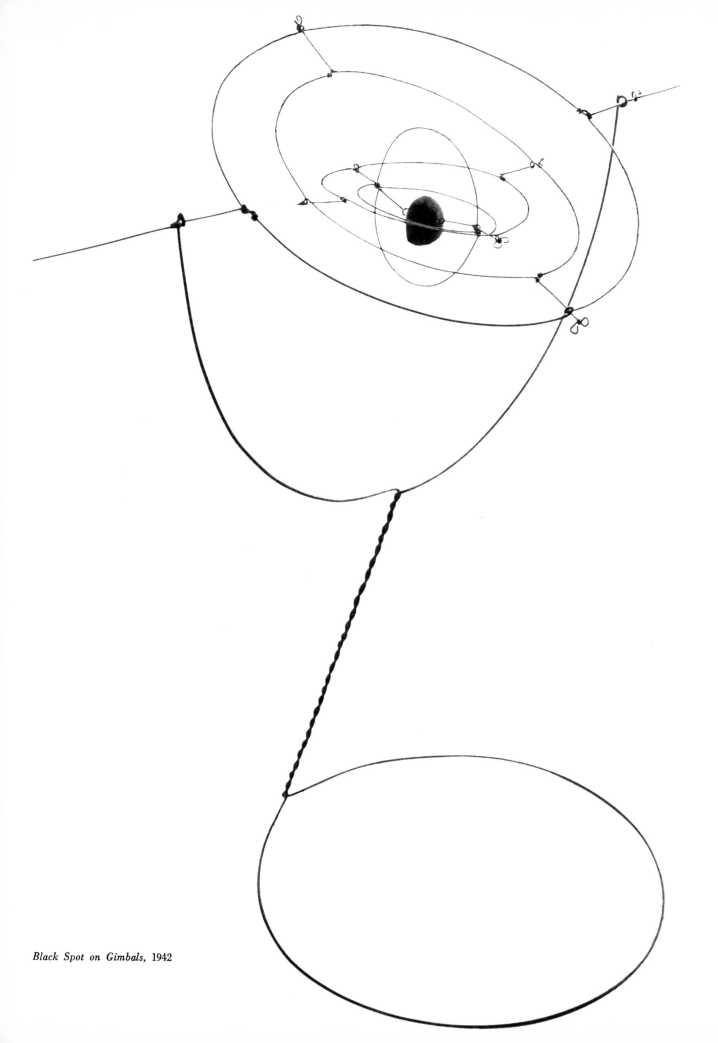

Black Spot on Gimbals, 1942

pedo jigs back and forth and the white sphere vibrates. A similar idea was used in 1938 as a model for a proposed large-scale motorized mobile for the 1939 New York World's Fair. This consisted of four upright elements of painted or polished metal: a corkscrew, two elements made up of balanced segments from circles, and a diamond shape set on a base. All of these again rotated on turntables.

The *Four Elements* in Stockholm is actually an enlargement of a second model made in 1938 for the 1939 World's Fair. This is installed outside the Moderna Museet there, and attains a height of 30 feet. A great black bastion has a pointed oval table top which rolls back and forth on its base. An orange figure motif with outflung, arched arms whirls round and round. The tallest element is a simple black and white pole with an orange disk at the end of an arm set at right angles, which revolves slowly. The fourth element again consists of a column of diminishing segments from circles, painted orange and yellow. All four elements have separate motors which permit of considerable variation in the movements.

Calder was also commissioned to create a fountain, *Water Ballet*, for the exhibition hall of the New York Consolidated Edison Company at the 1939 World's Fair. As a result of technical problems this was not put into operation at the time; however, he was enabled to recreate it in 1954 for the architect Eero Saarinen's General Motors Technological Center in Detroit. This fountain is a complex interaction of moving jets of water which function as the mobile unit. Although the design of fountains would seem to be an inevitable development of the mobile concept, Calder has had very few commissions for them.

The most important is the recently completed fountain (1964) for the new building of the Los Angeles County Museum. This consists of a group of standing mobiles, standing on simple high, triangular-shaped bases. Long crossbars support large flat blades, circular and free-form. In order to achieve visibility across one of the adjoining buildings the artist extended two of the arms high in the air in a gesture of gay greeting. This gave to the entire structure the name, *Hello Girls!* Jets of water striking the blades whirl the mobiles, and the water power justifies the classification of the fountain with the mechanical mobiles.

Hello Gir

VII   The Great Mobiles

As previously noted, the war years brought forth a number of other experimental forms, notably the series of wood and wire constructions which Calder named *Constellations*. The name was obviously suggested by the manner in which the carved wooden shapes were grouped and joined by their wires; the general concept as well as the name may have been suggested by some painted *Constellations* which Miró had produced a few years earlier.

The *Constellations* of Calder are principally stabiles, extremely beautiful and delicate, and highly finished in the working of the mostly organic, wooden shapes. They are of interest both in terms of their own exquisite quality and also as assimilations of the very first geometric, wire stabiles of 1931 to the organic shapes which have marked his mature style. Also, they represent his last serious exploration of wood carving, at this stage carried out in terms of abstract shapes frequently suggestive of those of Arp. With the exception of one or two related pieces such as *Wood Objects on Wood Post*, dated 1947, Calder did not pursue the theme of the *Constellations* after 1944.

Another short-lived experiment of the war years was carried out in the area of bronze casting. Although a few of his earliest figurative sculptures had been cast in bronze, Calder had actually modelled very little in clay or plaster during his career. A fear that he might become enslaved to his materials of sheet metal and wood led him, about the time of his exhibition at The Museum of Modern Art, New York, to attempt some works in plaster, to be cast in bronze. The nature of the material led to a temporary return to a form of representation, although generally in a satiric vein and at a considerable remove from reality.

Of those plasters which were cast in bronze, among the most successful are *Snake on the Arch* and *Double Helix*, both dated 1944.

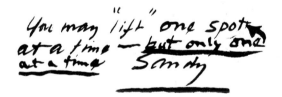

These may be classified as standing mobiles, involving a precise balance of elements to create relatively simple movements which are, however, given a particular dignity and emphasis because of the ease and grace with which the quite apparently heavy material is made to rotate or undulate. Whether the experiments with the *Constellations* and plaster modelling and bronze casting served any useful purpose as a catharsis, it is difficult to say. All that is certain is that by the end of the

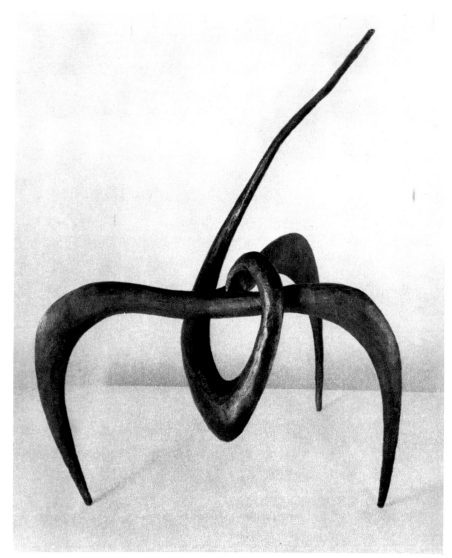

Snake on the Arch, 1944

Double Helix, 1944

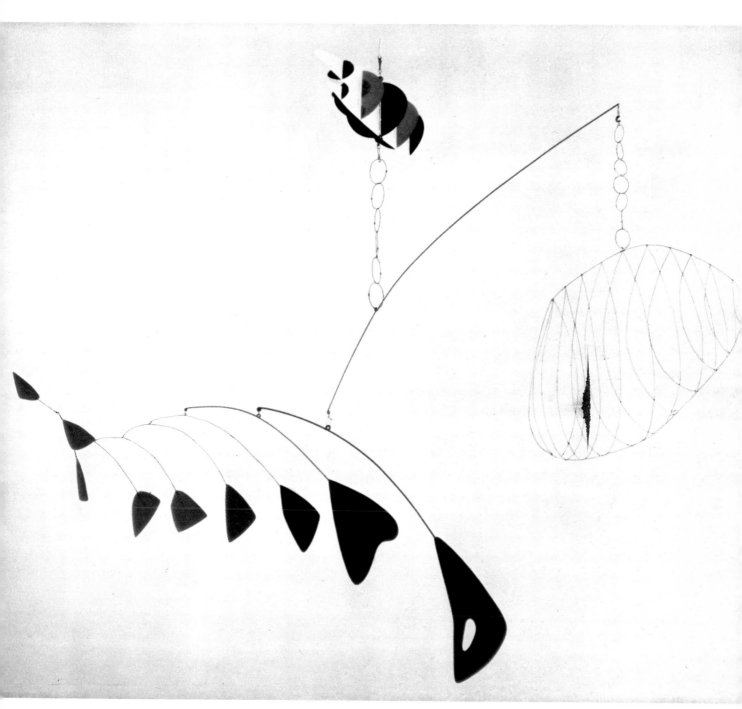

Lobster Trap and Fish Tail, 1939, Collection The Museum of Modern Art, New York. Gift of the Advisory Committee.

Spider, 1939

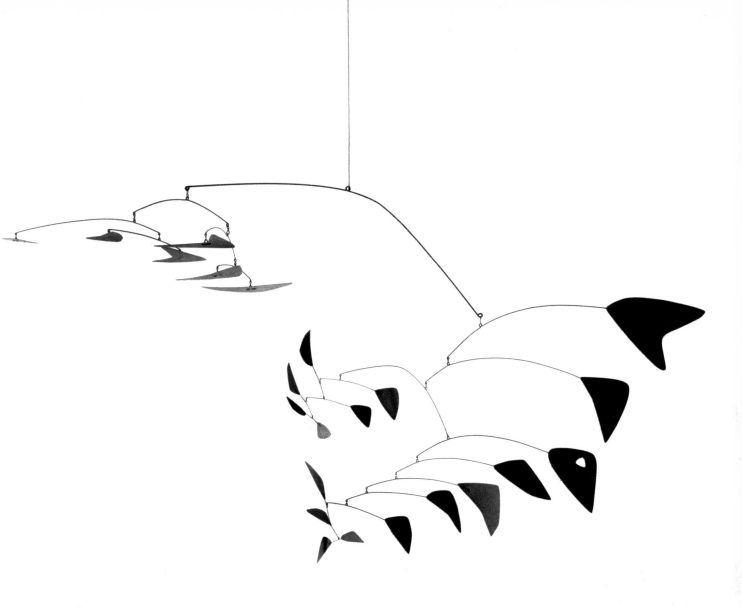

Roxbury Red, 1963

war Calder had once more turned all his energies to metal construction and had entered upon the most fertile and imaginative period of his creative life.

The post-war years between 1945 and 1950 saw the resumption of the artist's contacts with Europe and a continual increase in his world-wide reputation. His works were exhibited regularly in the United States and in France; other exhibitions were held in Holland, Switzerland, and Rio de Janeiro and São Paulo in Brazil. A large mobile was commissioned for Cincinnati, a motion picture was made about him, and in 1950 a retrospective of his sculptures was organized at Massachusetts Institute of Technology.

Special exhibitions, prizes, awards, and other honors, commissions and a frantic competition for his works by museums and collectors throughout the world have marked a triumphant progress by Calder through the fifties and sixties. However, all these outward manifestations of recognition and success have at no point impeded or delayed his own work, either in terms of its incredible quantity or the continual imaginative development which he displays as he has come to full maturity as an artist.

The late forties and the fifties saw the flowering of the mobiles, both in their hanging versions, and increasingly in variants which might be standing on a base or attached to a wall. During the same period, the artist was becoming more and more interested in forms of sheet-metal stabiles. With a few notable exceptions such as *Whale*, 1937, and *Black Beast*, 1940, the earlier stabiles were generally created on a relatively modest scale. From these, however, there were ultimately to emerge the tremendous, monumental stabiles of the sixties, some of the most impressive and important works of the artist's career.

In the hanging mobiles there was constant experimentation with the possibilities of spatial movement of the widest possible variety.

The largest number of these continued to be produced on a scale suitable to be hung within a normal-sized room. However, there is apparent from the late forties forward a growing interest in the creation of monumental forms, the transformation of the mobile from an intimate object, characterized by lightness and emphasis on linear patterns, to great architectural-sculptural wind machines, whose powerful but precisely balanced metal rods, tipped with large, flat, organically shaped

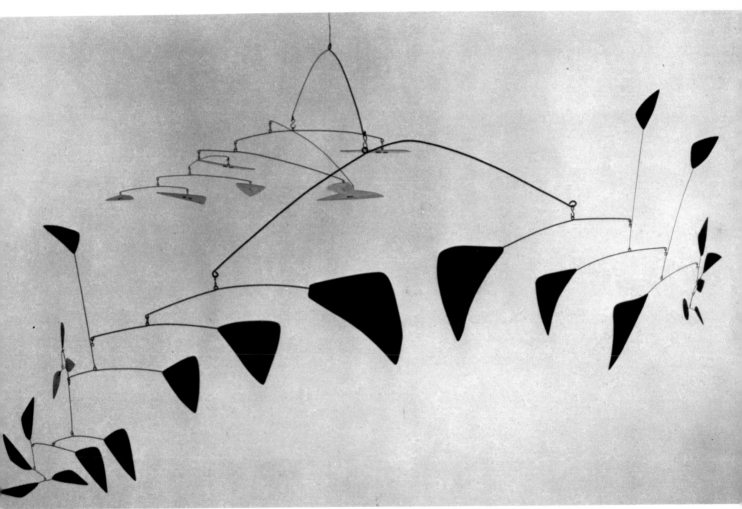

Sumac, 1961

disks, encompass and define vast areas of architectural space. The difficulty with the monumental hanging mobile is that of finding an appropriate space in which to install it. Even in large public buildings or museums there is not too frequently the sort of free and uncluttered space suitable to a really large-scale mobile; and in the early fifties very few architects were actually considering appropriate works of painting or sculpture in the initial stages of their architectural design.

Thus the opportunities for large-scale commissions of mobiles were relatively scarce, and if Calder wanted to work on a monumental scale, he must at first gamble on his own experiments. This he did with a few very large hanging mobiles, such as the all-white *International Mobile* created in 1949 for the great staircase of the Philadelphia Museum, but not accepted, and then loaned to various museums in the hope that they might find a space in which it could be permanently installed. It finally found a most congenial home in Mies van der Rohe's Cullinan Hall of the Museum of Fine Arts, Houston. However, of necessity most of the hanging mobiles have continued to be of manageable proportions, although during the latter fifties and early sixties an increasing number of even the non-commissioned ones have grown in general diameter to proportions of ten, fifteen, and sometimes thirty feet, with proportionate increase in the scale of all the elements.

One of the largest hanging mobiles of the thirties is *Lobster Trap and Fish Tail*, 1939, with a widest diameter of some fifteen feet, which hangs in the stair well of The Museum of Modern Art, New York. The delicacy of the elements, however, somewhat disguises the actual size. This is a work of considerable beauty and of interest in a variety of ways. While it is actually quite abstract in all its forms, it embodies an extremely strong sense of literal subject in terms of its various associations. The topmost element is a curious looking, torpedo-shaped object which could be the lobster cautiously approaching the trap, represented by a delicate wire cage balancing at one end of the crossbar. Around the other end is clustered a group of fan-shaped metal plates suggestive of a school of fish.

The strong subject content is also apparent in another very different and much smaller mobile produced the following year, *Snake and the Cross*, c. 1940, an unusual and experimental work consisting simply of two pro-

78

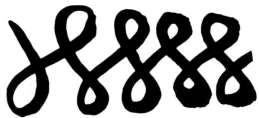

portionately large forms. The cross embodies two oval shapes, orange and yellow, interpenetrating at right angles. Hovering over this cross is a loosely ambiguous black shape which, on examination, takes on the appearance of a cobra head poised to strike. The mobile composition with only two or three large simple forms balanced against one another was repeated again in *The Gong*, which is merely an orange disk or gong hanging at one end of a horizontal bar, the other end of which is a wooden ball, giving it the appearance of a drumstick. The entire unit is balanced at the other end of the central crossbar by a vaguely ovoid black shape. Such simple mobiles are limited in terms of their possibilities of motion, and it may be for this reason that Calder did not pursue this direction. *The Gong* did, however, have a particular importance for some later mobiles in that it suggested the possibility of adding, through actual metal gongs and hammers, the element of sound to that of motion.

The variations on the types of hanging mobiles are so great that it is almost impossible to categorize them, and the actual number produced by the artist during the last twenty years is so vast that they almost defy the cataloguer. A few of the more characteristic types may be described in order to suggest the range of possibilities which Calder has explored in the forms of the mobile. *Five Red Arcs*, which dates about 1948, belongs to the most delicate and open type, with long, free, crossrods at the ends of which are balanced three rather simple groups, one of small white disks, one of the five red crescent or arc shapes, and one of some varied geometric shapes, triangular or diamond. The entire effect of a mobile such as this is that of the most extreme airy lightness; the space which it occupies is defined by the barest minimum of lines and solid shapes.

The Forest in the Best Place, c. 1945, now in Stockholm, is a radically different hanging mobile, and one which in many ways is more pertinent to the artist's subsequent development. This may be described as a vertical mobile, extending ten feet from ceiling almost to the floor in two or three great, sweeping curves. The upper part consists of seven large leaf forms arranged in a vertical pattern; the lower part, also of large, simple shapes, is arranged in a horizontal emphasis. The whole is painted black, a tendency which increases in the later works, particularly in the stabiles.

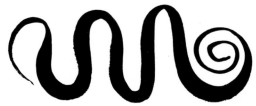

The denial of color is related to the search for simple monumentality, as though the bright, gay colors have an association of the elegant and the decorative which Calder wished to eliminate. *Black Mobile with Hole*, 1954, combines some of the characteristics of the previous two. Its dimensions of approximately seven by nine feet (outside circumference) places it between the two in scale. Its general character involves a combination of upper vertical emphasis and lower horizontal. The leaf-shaped plaques range from large upper ones to small lower ones, several of them cut out to increase the feeling of lightness and spatial penetration. This belongs to the more naturalistic wing, suggestive of flowers swaying at the end of long stems.

Periodically Calder turns back to the regular geometric shapes, principally circular disks, which marked his very first excursions into abstraction. He has also, in recent years, produced a number of hanging mobiles in which the emphasis is predominantly horizontal, with the color shapes arranged over a wide area but in relatively narrow depth, to create a pattern extending over a large part of a ceiling but still staying well within the upper part of a room of normal height. *Red Lily Pads*, 1956, illustrates this direction although on a scale more monumental (c. seventeen feet horizontally by c. four feet vertically) than most of the mobiles of this type. In this he has limited himself to related red shapes which vary slightly from the circle,

all of which float horizontally in a manner appropriate to lily pads floating on the surface of a pond. The free leaf-form still, perhaps, remains his favorite, obviously because it is capable of so many variations and since the leaf at the end of the branch-like wire rod takes on a naturalistic association from which the artist never wishes to depart for very long.

Two of the most recent hanging mobiles are closely associated in their general organization, although the colors give to each of them a quite distinct character. *Roxbury Red*, 1963, harks back in its general arrangement to *Black Mobile with Hole*, although the brilliant red color changes its character, and the main groupings are reversed, with a horizontal arrangement of the upper elements and vertical of the lower. Leaf, fan, and crescent-shaped metal disks perpetuate the feeling of delicate, living plant life. *Ghost*, 1964, was designed as the key piece for the retrospective at the Guggenheim Museum, and is one of the largest and most impressive hanging mobiles ever created by the artist, measuring some 24 by 35 feet. It was designed to hang from the central dome of the Guggenheim Museum. In order that it might not interfere unduly with the other works of art arranged around the ramps, which could be viewed from across the central void, Calder deliberately made the work extremely light in proportions, airy and delicate in feeling, and painted it white so that it might assimilate more easily to the complicated architectural environment.

Model for *Ghost*, 1964

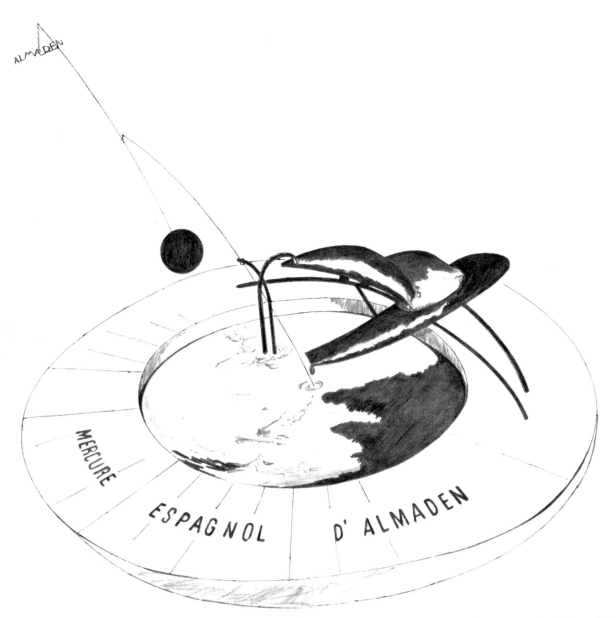

Mercury Fountain, 1937 (Drawing by William Stitt)

VIII Commissioned Works

During the fifties the artist did receive some commissions for monumental works, although most of these were for standing mobiles. Commissions for stabiles have proliferated during the last two or three years. His first really important commission had been the *Mercury Fountain* for the Spanish Pavilion of the Paris Exposition of 1937. The Spanish Pavilion was designed by the architects José Luis Sert and Luis Lacasa, with mural decorations by Picasso and Miró. The fountain, designed by Calder at the invitation of Sert, consisted of a large concrete basin, lined with pitch to resist the corrosion by the mercury. Calder painted his construction black with pitch for the same purpose, and possibly the idea of using black for his monumental sculpture was first suggested by this work. The fountain which he constructed is best described as a form of standing mobile, with the mercury flowing through a series of open troughs into the pool, and a long crossbar rising above and balancing a metal disk against the lettered name of the source for the mercury, Almaden.

The *Mercury Fountain* was a relatively simple structure, not much advanced technically or aesthetically beyond the *Steel Fish* of 1934. However, it was Calder's first major commission and a successful one, so that it en-

couraged him greatly in the exploration of the monumental possibilities of his sculptural forms.

Unfortunately, subsequent commissions were few and far between for the next fifteen years. The designs for the New York World's Fair were never realized at the time. A large, although not monumental mobile was commissioned for the Terrace Hotel in Cincinnati, in 1946. Then in 1952 the artist received his greatest commission to date, the design of an acoustical ceiling for an auditorium in University City, Caracas. The entire ceiling is broken up by Calder with gigantic, brightly colored free shapes, which seem to float in mid-air and which immensely enhance the architectural space of the interior. Also, astonishingly, the shapes function beautifully as far as the acoustic properties of the hall are concerned.

In 1957 a giant mobile was commissioned for Idlewild (now Kennedy) Airport in New York. This huge, simple structure, with very large leaf blades painted red and black with one orange accent, is placed in a vast hall, the upper part of which is open with many windows, but not cluttered with too many architectural details. Thus it provides a favorable if not ideal setting for Calder's greatest hang-

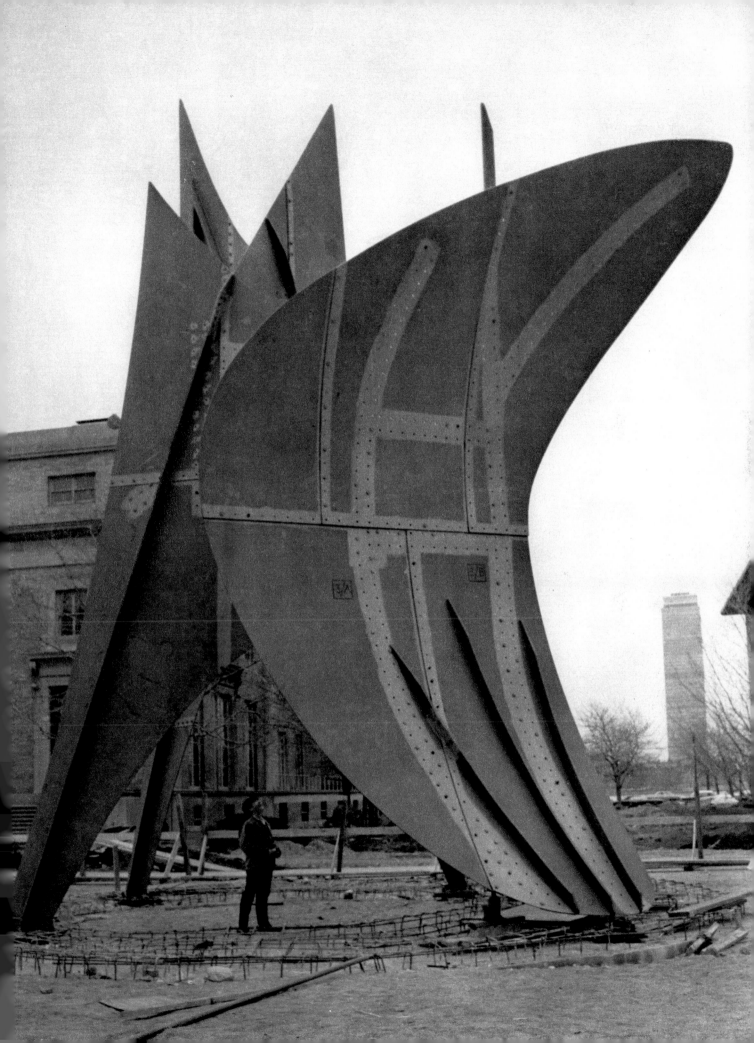

ing mobile to date. The combination of mobile and architecture which is achieved here is a unique demonstration of the tremendous possibilities of the mobile form, conceived and executed on this scale, for really monumental expression.

The difficulty, as always, is that in order to achieve an ideal marriage, it would be necessary for Calder to work with an architect from the beginning. It might be necessary for the architect to make some adjustments in his concepts of his architectural space, and this is not too easy to persuade an architect to do. Thus, as far as the hanging mobiles at least are concerned, Calder seems fated to continue to suffer the fate of being forced to design them for already predetermined spaces. Fortunately, he is always cheerfully willing to do this, and when given the opportunity inevitably shows the greatest ingenuity in overcoming architectural difficulties without in any way compromising his own design.

Acoustic Ceiling, 1952, Aula Magna, University City, Caracas

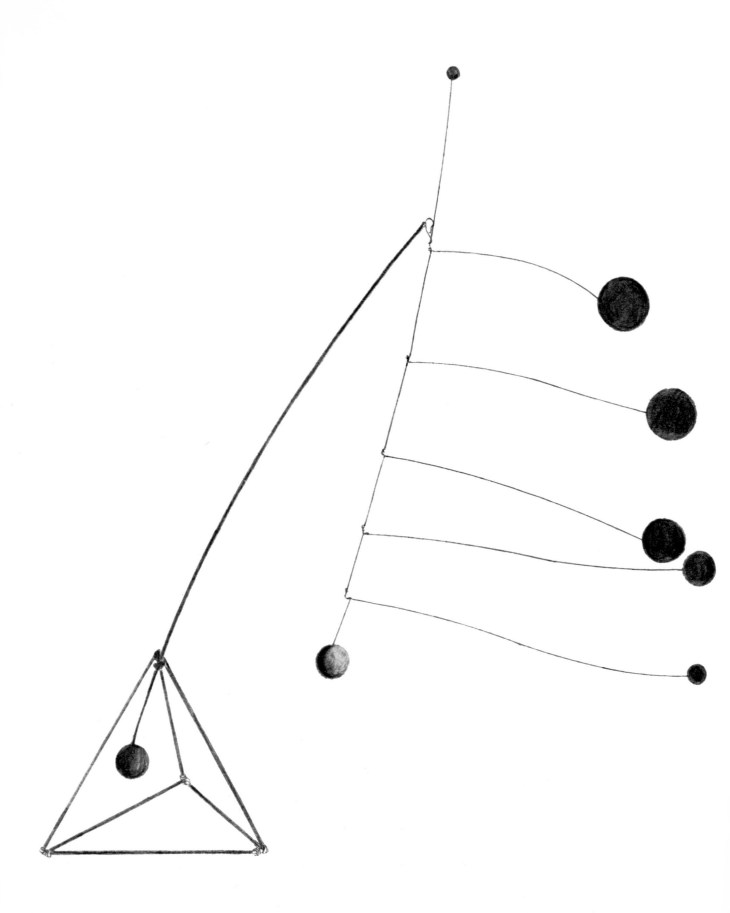

Calderberry Bush, 1932
(Drawing by William Stitt)

IX   Standing Mobiles

The standing mobile actually antedated the hanging mobile in Calder's work. The first wire goldfish bowl was a sort of standing mobile, and *Calderberry Bush*, dated in 1932, discussed above, stated succinctly and in a most accomplished fashion many of the principles of this form. Obviously the standing mobile, in which the mobile unit was attached to a simple framework base, had its roots more clearly in the history of past sculpture and also was a form more easily adaptable to the exigencies of installation than the hanging mobile. Since the mobile, powered by currents of air, could function more easily outdoors than indoors, Calder began very early to explore the possibilities for outside mobiles.

Again, these could best be resolved in terms of some sort of standing mobile. The first on a large scale was *Steel Fish*, 1934, which also in its ten-foot height was the first attempt of the artist at monumental abstract sculpture. *Steel Fish* is made up of only a few large shapes, balanced on the most rudimentary iron bars. The largest, the torpedo-shaped fish, is attached by a vertical bar to the upper half-circle. The other elements are merely two disks and a hanging ball arranged in a tri-angulation of steel rods. The entire structure relates closely to the first wire stabiles exhibited at the Galerie Percier in 1931, with the

variations of the fish form and of motion. At the other end of the thirties it has certain associations with the *Lobster Trap and Fish Tail*, and in another context might be regarded as an abstraction of the first mechanized *Fishbowl with Crank*, 1929.

The artist's early exploration of the possibilities of monumental expression for his various sculptural forms may be illustrated by a number of other key works of the thirties and early forties. In another standing mobile, *Spherical Triangle*, 1939, eight feet high, he places a group of variously shaped, large curved triangular forms on a base bent from a single heavy iron rod. This, like the *Steel Fish* and virtually all the large metal-plate stabiles, is painted a uniform black. The denial of strongly contrasting colors in these earthbound sculptures, as suggested, would seem to be a deliberate statement by the artist as to their essentially sculptural nature. Also painted a uniform black were *Whale*, 1937, and *Black Beast*, 1940, two of the most impressive of the early metal-plate stabiles,

Black Beast, 1940

Whale, 1937, Collection The Museum of Modern Art, New York. Gift of the artist.

and two works which in many ways summarize the basic directions of the great stabiles of the early sixties, which constitute the most important body of monumental sculptures produced by the artist during his entire life. Both of these stabiles illustrate the techniques which Calder was to employ in most of his subsequent large-scale stabiles.

Each work consists of a number of plates of heavy steel, cut into fantastic organic or architectural forms, set into one another at various angles and then securely bolted. The technique is that of the industrial iron worker, except that Calder has normally used bolts which can be easily unscrewed, so that the large pieces can be taken apart to facilitate transportation and installation. The black paint is of no particular brand or quality. When it has weathered or discolored as the result of exposure outdoors, it merely needs another coat, and the artist has no objection if this is applied by any competent local painter. He himself, as the quantity and scale of his works have increased in recent years, now works with a crew of professional metal workers. Most of his large-scale stabiles are designed as miniature models, and then the large metal sheets are cut and formed by workmen at a foundry with, however, every detail supervised by the artist.

Whale is the pioneer example of that type of monumental stabile embodying fantastic, curvilinear shapes, suggestive of some swimming, writhing monster. Fins jut out at right angles from the central sheet, which may be the beast's body, and all the forms suggest violent activity, although of course nothing actually moves. This work is the ancestor of an entire progeny of bizarre stabiles, suggestive of perverted or monstrous animal or plant life. It is perhaps not incomprehensible that some of the most monumental works should be captioned after whales. One of the most recent and gayest of the large stabiles, in this case brilliantly colored, is appropriately named *Pregnant Whale.*

The second of the early large-scale stabiles is very different in character, although it also is intended to suggest some strange monster. *Black Beast,* 1940, which measures some nine by fourteen feet is made up of four large cutout plates intersecting at extreme angles. These, however, are shaped to create an open structure, with voids below as well as above, and the entire structure joined only at a narrow waist. There are suggestions of heads and legs attached to torsos, so that the animal changes from various views to a group of animals or to animals and human figures. The shapes are more rectilinear than is the case with *Whale,* and despite the beast connotation, the whole has a strongly architectural effect. It is this suggestion of sculpture which becomes an architectural environment that

makes *Black Beast* an important prototype for another major group of the most recent stabiles.

As was the case with the hanging mobiles, most of the standing mobiles of the forties and fifties were on a modest scale. In them the artist was able to explore a number of new variations on the possibilities of movement. Those on a simple, shaped wire base tended to the expression of linear patterns and a sort of vibrating, shimmering activity. An example is *Beggar's Penny*, 1962. Occasionally this type of all-wire standing mobile made the artist recall his very first wire stabiles of 1930-1931, and he reverted to pure geometric forms in mechanical if not mechanized motion (*Black Spot on Gimbals*, 1942, *Red Pyramid*, 1951). The *Towers*, created about 1951, constitute another type of standing or wall mobiles which are related to the first stabiles but which also represent a potentially important new direction which Calder abandoned and which he has not as yet resumed. These are architectural constructions, formed of wire frames defining a triangular or irregular rectangular tower shape, whose volume is further accented by occasional flat, colored slabs. Some mobile elements are usually attached to the top. The tower normally leans in a somewhat crazy zigzag, with a reminiscence of Delaunay's paintings of the Eiffel Tower.

The possibility of developing the standing mobile on a more monumental scale continued to intrigue him, and this led to a number of new formal experiments in this genre. One of the earliest with significant implications for the future is *Red Petals* 1942. This is an immensely graceful, naturalistic form, in every detail suggestive of some exotic plant or tree. The base consists of a tripod of three triangular leaf forms, resting on their points and supporting a tall, curving stem some nine feet high, from whose very tip extend the most delicate tendrils of wires balancing leaf or flower shapes. The importance of this work lies not only in its scale and its organic beauty, but in the statement of the standing mobile as an organic whole, consisting of interrelated stabile and mobile forms and not simply as a mobile attached to a base. This is a formula the implications of which Calder has yet to realize fully.

A different but equally significant solution for the standing mobile is to be seen in such a work as *Lily of Force*, 1944. In this work the mobile elements predominate and the stabile base is subordinated to a very low, almost ground-level unit which serves only to anchor the whole to the ground. Above the base, a

Yellow Disc, 1953

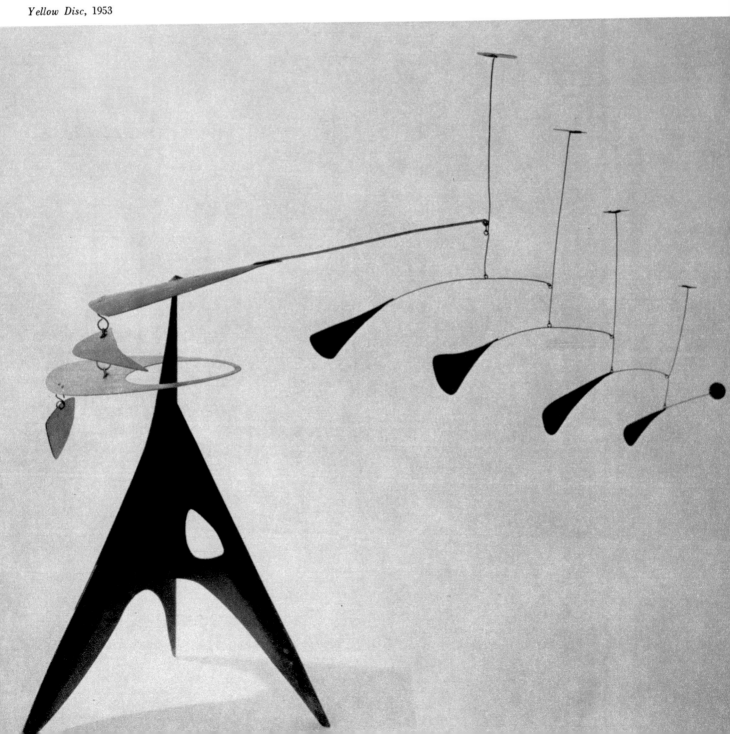

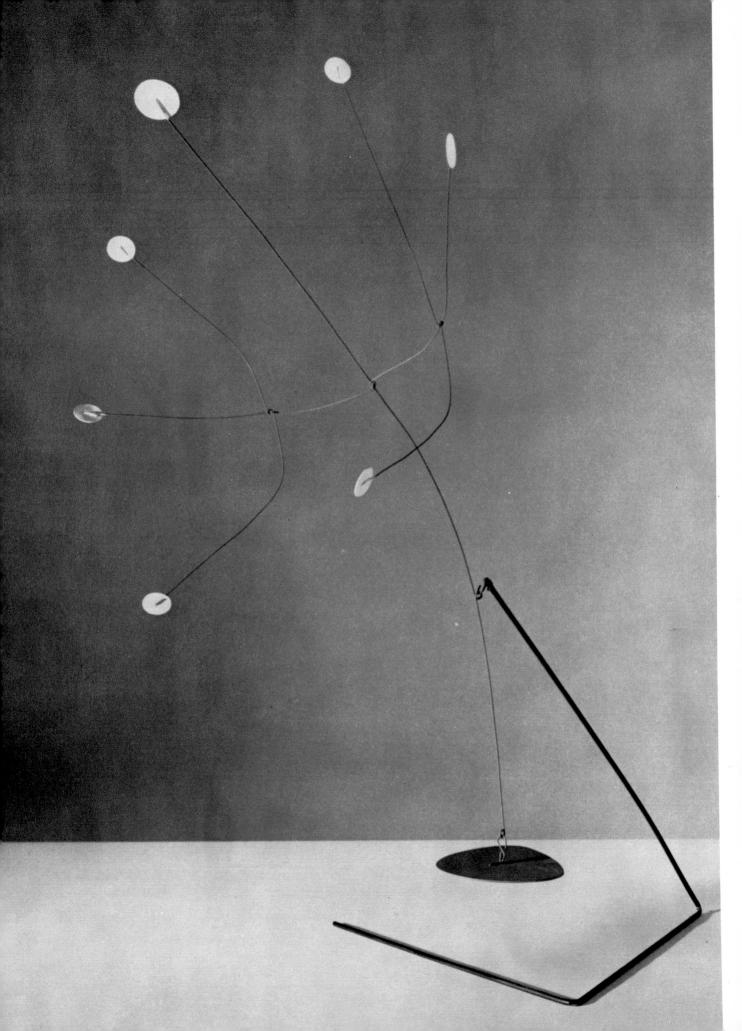

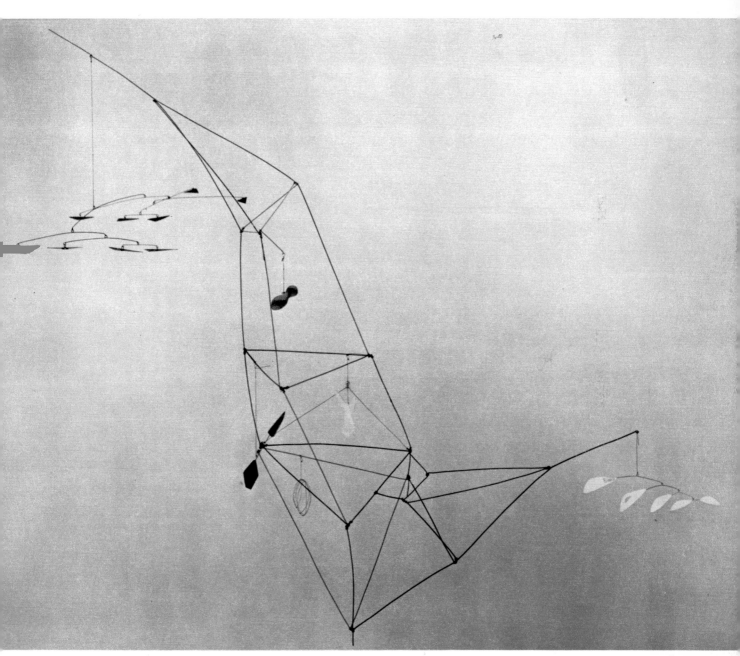

wer, 1951

ggar's Penny, 1962

large, free-form, horizontal, mobile plate, with cut-out holes, acts as a single counterbalance to all the other delicate elements of the construction. Out of the holes grow long tendrils of wire, jointed at several points, to which are attached varicolored leaf forms. The structure is capable of a wide variety of movements, circular and undulating and always suggestive of the living plant forms to which it owes its genesis. Despite its radically different appearance, it is a development of the structural principles first stated in 1932 in *Calderberry Bush.*

Yellow Disk, 1953, presents some of the aspects of both *Red Petals* and of *Lily of Force.* A high tripod base comes to a single upper point which penetrates a horizontal oval disk. This, supported by two smaller shapes, balances the short arm of a long, horizontal unit. At the pointed end of the longer arms there extends a cluster of leaves on wire tendrils. The motion is again a simple circular rotation of the leaves around the tripod base, with the penetrated disk revolving in its own central orbit. *Yellow Disk*, with a series of variations, suggests the form which many of the most monumental standing mobiles were to assume during the fifties and sixties.

A principal characteristic of these large standing mobiles has been the statement of the stabile portion essentially as a base, rather than as an independent stabile sculpture. It would be natural to assume that the monumental standing mobiles should inevitably combine the characteristics of the hanging mobile with those of the stabile. However, the artist has (with a few exceptions) resisted the temptation to combine the two forms, and in most versions has attempted to create an independent construction which is distinct from either. It is perhaps indicative of his attitude that he resents and resists the label "stabile-mobile" or "mobile-stabile" which is sometimes attached to these seemingly combined works. To him they are mobiles standing on a base, at least in most of the versions which he has created to date. Certain recent variants may indicate a modification in this attitude.

Calder's approach to this problem has not been absolutely consistent, any more than any immensely creative artist's approach can be consistent. *El Corcovado*, 1951 (c. eleven feet high, Collection José Luis Sert) which is one of the earlier developed standing mobiles on a large scale, has a monumental and varied geometric base which could exist independently as a stabile. In *Whirling Ear*, the standing mobile created for the United States Pavilion of the Brussels World's Fair in 1957, he combines a single great pennant form with a three-dimensional, highly sculptural base on

which it revolves majestically. This is a late mechanized mobile and might be considered as a sort of 'sport,' since it does not seem to relate to anything the artist has done before or since.

On the other hand, a whole group of large standing mobiles, created in the last few years, function as mobile units rotating in a limited but impressive movement, over a generally pyramidal base which is essentially neutral in its plastic form. These would include *The Spiral* created for the UNESCO building in Paris in 1958, *Lollypops*, dated 1962, *Five Rudders*, 1964, and *Sandy's Butterfly*, 1964. The last is the climax of this particular form, a massive structure with a bright red, pyramidal base on whose apex are balanced, with incredible delicacy, crossrods bearing enormous, heavy leaves, which move with a slow but easy dignity.

A group of standing mobiles created in the last few years suggest that the artist may be re-examining this position, and searching for a more complete integration of the mobile and stabile concepts. The most impressive of these is *Southern Cross*, 1963, which stands 24 feet high. Although the stabile element, still painted in bright orange, functions as a base with four long, curving, animal-like legs (above which rises a vertical beam, to the top of which the horizontal mobile elements are attached) the proportions of base to mobile are reversed in scale, to make the stabile more prominent than the mobile. A small model of *Southern Cross* gives even more importance to the wide-spread legs, relating them strongly to some of the major architectural stabiles of recent years. This pattern is obviously being explored by the artist in a number of models for standing mobiles created recently, in which greater and greater variety, both in shape and color, is being lavished on the stabile portions (*Crinkly*, 1964, *Crinkly with Five Rudders*, 1964).

At various times Calder has created wall stabiles or wall mobiles involving stabile elements. Many of the *Constellations* and *Towers*

could be classified in these fashions. Another group which was a product of the fifties seems to represent something of a relaxation from his more serious investigations of monumental mobile and stabile forms and also, in a lighter vein, a more literal re-examination of subject.

Five Rudders, 1964

Crinkly with Five Rudders, 1964

Crinkly, 1964

These are usually on a modest scale, ranging from 20 to 60 inches, maximum diameter. Two black wall stabiles dated 1952 and 1954 are entitled *Escutcheon*, but their impact is rather protozoic than heraldic. In the first, two large amoeba shapes with cut-out centers overlap each other, while around their periphery cluster groups of smaller shapes, like sperm fertilizing ova, from one of which there shoots out a wire tendril joining it to another small disk. In the other, the wires proliferate, with graduated objects scattered along them as if creeping towards the matrix forms.

The *Escutcheons* suggest most specifically some forms of microscopic organisms, but most of the later works in this group are definitely related to fish and other kinds of marine life. *Flying Fish*, 1957, is a black, hanging mobile fish-form, all gaping mouth and fluttering fins. *Eyes and Feather*, 1958, could by the title be some gaily-colored form of bird life, but the eyes, the general contours, and the floating tendrils again suggest the fishy breed. *Yellow Whale*, 1958, is treated much more abstractly than the ones mentioned, with its large, irregular body shape supporting mobile elements of graceful black leaves and one red disk. *Red Head*, 1958, reverts to a particularly stupid-looking animal or fish head. *Black Sponge*, 1958, is a wall mobile, a delicate version of the *Lily of Force type*.

Fishy, 1952, might best be described as a crawling mobile, since the elements, stabile and mobile, are loosely scattered over the wall to suggest a large blue and large yellow fish pursuing a school of small black fish. In this group of mobiles of the fifties in which the artist re-explores some aspects of humorous representation the influence of Miro seems particularly strong. There are many reminiscences of little beasts or microorganisms that suggests the Spanish painter in his lighter vein. For Calder these works represent a sort of catharsis, an unburdening of the load of facetiousness which he can never entirely get rid of, and which sometimes disturbs even his most serious works.

Normally he works off the excess in the toys and gadgets or miniature mobiles with which he continually occupies his spare time, but occasionally he apparently needs to perpetrate what might be described as more serious works in a literal and humorous vein. In them he created a delightful lot of little monsters, animal, marine, or insect life, filled with a spirit of spontaneous and colorful enthusiasm, hanging or crawling stabiles and mobiles which, in effect, were joyous caricatures of his own production. These gay if no less serious excursions into subject formed the immediate background of the great stabiles of the early sixties.

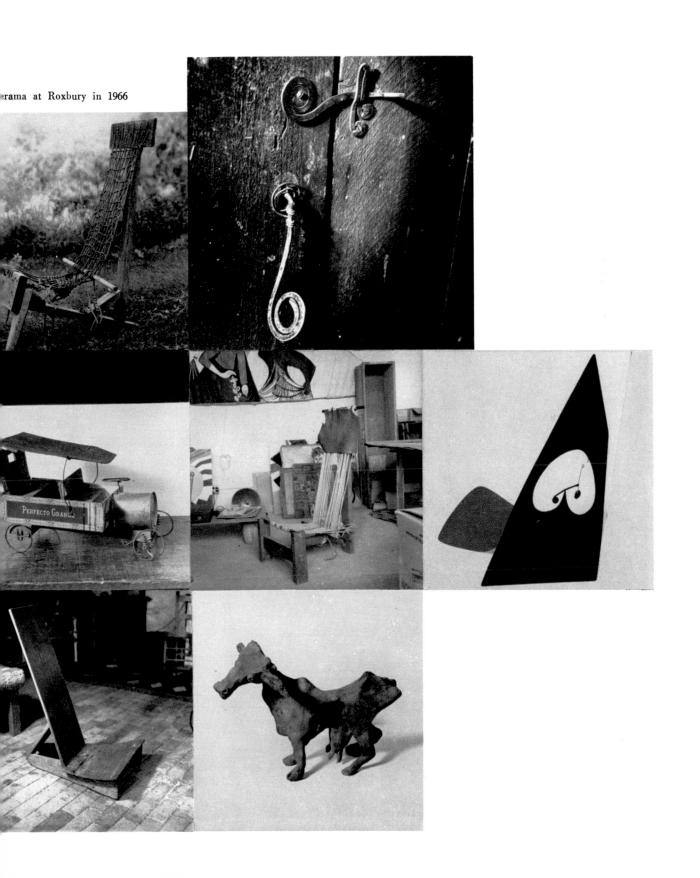

rama at Roxbury in 1966

X The Great Stabiles

Whereas the standing mobiles of Calder may be only at the inception of their potential development, the most impressive achievement of the artist during the sixties unquestionably is to be found in his great stabiles. Presumably any piece of sculpture which does not actually move may be described as a stabile. Thus, all sculptures before Calder from the beginning of time, with a few exceptions, were stabiles. However, the term really belongs to him and even within his total work has a particular application to the large-scale metal plate constructions, normally painted black, which are identified with him and with nobody else. Even the original wire abstractions of the 1931 Galerie Percier exhibition, to which Jean Arp facetiously attached the name, seem less familiar to us under this description than under the constructivist term of 'wire construction.'

In any event the stabile in its developed and typical form may be said to have emerged with the *Whale* of 1937. In this work and in the 1940 *Black Beast* most of the characteristics of the monumental metal-plate stabile are apparent. In the early forties, under the wartime limitation on metals, he experimented with a number of small stabiles (*Black Thing* and *Spiny*, 1942) in which, perhaps because of their scale, he emphasized

qualities of grace and elegance. Although it is always difficult to establish an exact stylistic chronology for Calder's works (at least after the apprentice stage) there seems to have been a general exploration of qualities of delicacy and finish during the war period. This has been noted in the *Constellations*, in mobiles like *Spider*, 1939, or stabiles like *Morning Star*, 1943. This last work also, like a number of others at the same time, illustrates a re-exploration of some of the earlier qualities of pure geometry.

In the small stabiles the grace was characteristically expressed in architectural structural shapes which afforded the first glimpses of forms which only recently have been given their full, monumental expression. *Gothic Construction from Scraps*, 1939, has a most suggestive title, indicating its genesis in parings of metal left over from the cutting of large sheets. Out of these thin strips, which probably fell from the shears into a series of curving shapes, the artist created a cathedral which has all the open, structural character of thirteenth-century Gothic. In it we can already see one of those great environmental sculptures, created in the last two years, into which the spectator can actually walk. The feeling for a sort of romantic elegance is even apparent in the names which are given to

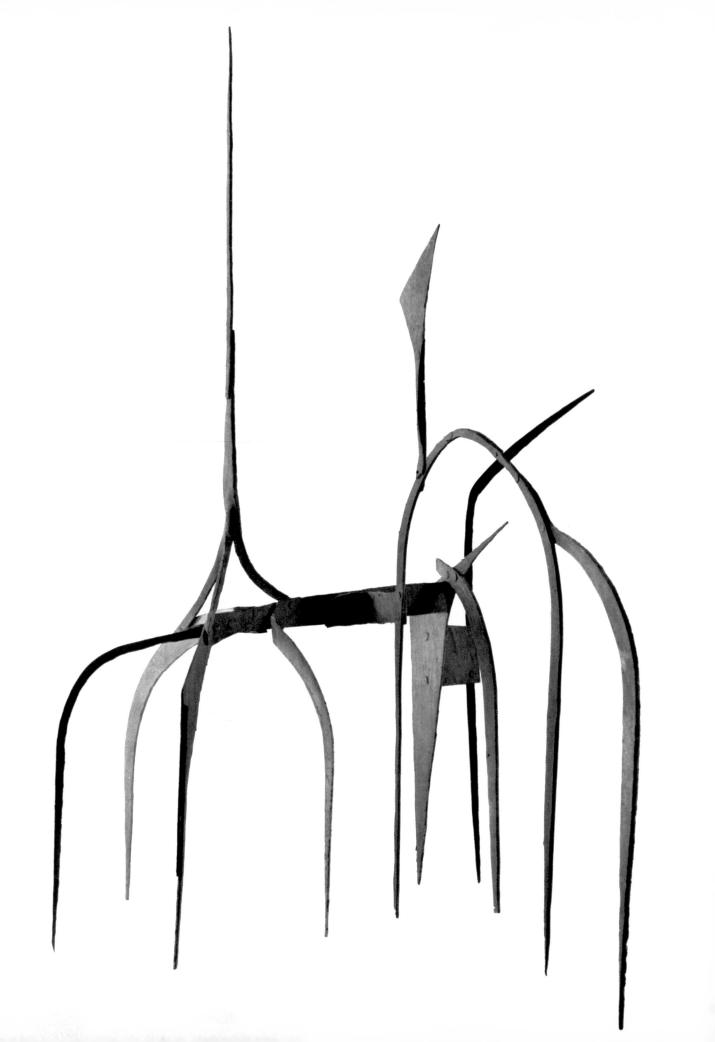

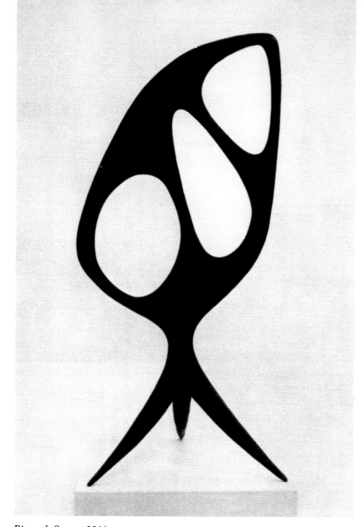

Pierced Stone, 1944

Morning Cobweb, 1945

c Construction from Scraps, 1939

some of these small stabiles. *Morning Cobweb*, 1945, is exactly that, a graceful linear structure of interlocking triangles.

With the end of the war the opportunity to create large-scale stabiles came once more, but the artist was involved in so many other projects that his exploration of this form was, with one or two exceptions, deferred. *Portrait of a Young Man*, 1945, although only thirty-five inches high, is monumental in conception, and revives the dada fantasy of organic shapes first suggested in the 1937 *Whale*. *Monocle*, 1948, of the same scale, belongs in the same vein of fantasy, extended here to include deliberate satire.

The large-scale metal-sheet stabile form was neglected by Calder during most of the fifties in his continuing search for new solutions in the mobile, and very few examples were produced over this ten-year period. His interest in stabiles was suddenly revived in the early sixties, with the result that the last few years have seen the sudden and tremendous flowering of the great, monumental stabiles which are some of the most impressive works of sculpture to be produced during the 20th century. One of the first of the new group is *Funghi Neri*, 1960, suggestive of three black standing figures closely related in shape and character to the figure-like elements of the 1940 *Black Beast*. The principal impetus for a new exploration of large-scale stabiles undoubtedly came about with the opportunity to design an immense version for the outdoor sculpture exhibition held in 1962 in Spoleto, Italy. The *Teodelapio* which he created for this occasion rises to a height of sixty feet, and one can drive a car through its arched shapes. With its arrow and spire pointing upward it is suggestive again of some Gothic structure, a vast expansion of the little *Gothic Construction* which had first been made from scraps of metal in 1939. Whether inspired by this achievement, the consequence of a natural development, or a maturation of ideas which had been simmering for over 20 years, during the last three years the artist has devoted his maximum energies to the production of one great stabile after another. These constitute so impressive an achievement that it is still difficult to evaluate their actual importance. Although, as suggested above, the new stabiles have their roots in many experiments which the artist carried on earlier in his life, in their realization they constitute an entire new chapter, almost an entire new style.

In the recent large stabiles Calder again demonstrates the range of his fertile mind. They assume all shapes from a highly simplified and functional-looking *Snowplow*, 1963, to a gay and ludicrous *Pregnant Whale*, 1963. However, two principal directions, broadly conceived, may again be noted in them. The first of these perpetuates the spirit of fantasy, expressed in more or less organic shapes, which first appeared on any scale in the sheet-metal stabile, *Whale*, in 1937. In another

w Plow, 1963

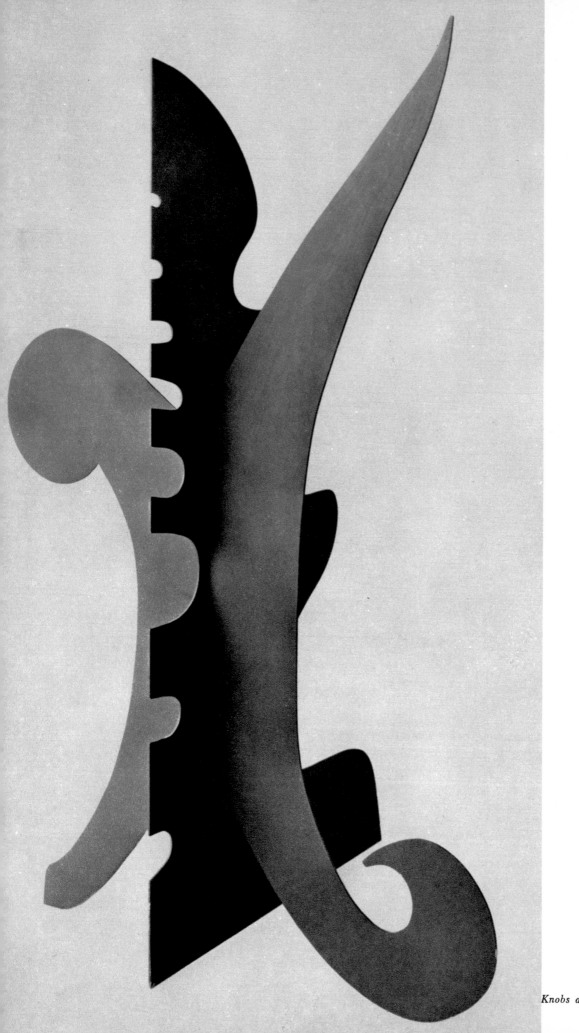

Portrait of a Young Man,

Knobs and Curlicues, 1963

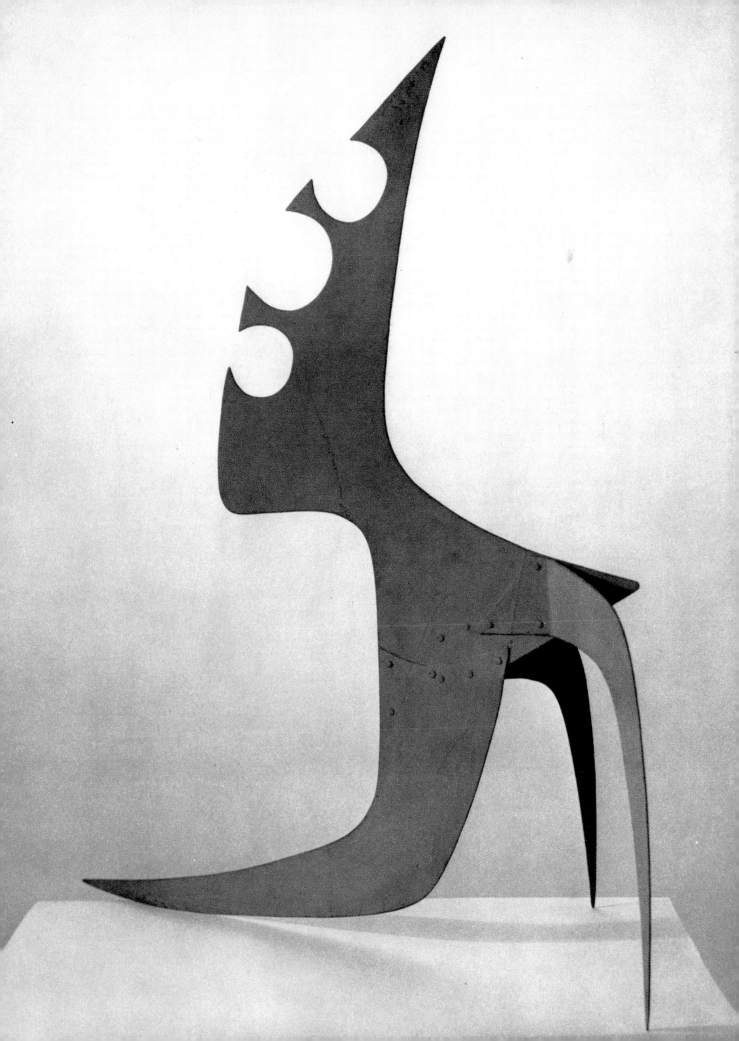

sense it could be said that this monstrous but not particularly menacing *Whale* and his spiritual descendants of 1963 and 1964, the stabiles *Knobs and Curlicues, Prickly Pear,* 1964, and *Octopus,* 1964, may all be traced back to the circus caricatures, the circus acrobats and animals, the wire caricatures, and all those early evidences of a delightful and often childlike humor which was the first form of aesthetic expression which the artist ever attempted. Posed on the grounds of Calder's Roxbury farm, the monsters spar and threaten each other in a manner that does not intimidate even the little children who run back and forth between them or climb over them.

The spirit of fantasy may also manifest itself in shapes that are geometric or rectilinear. The two *Jousting Knights,* 1963, enlarged from little toy figures to approximately six feet in height, combine loosely circular-shaped torsos with rigidly triangular legs in the creation of a splendid caricature of chivalry. *Polygon on Triangles (The Nun)* 1964, was simply a large abstract stabile made up of interlocked triangles when suddenly it transformed itself into a figure with a great, flying cowl and sweeping robes. Hence, *The Nun.*

The other major direction which may be noted among Calder's recent stabiles, and perhaps the one of most ultimate significance, is that which develops the theme of architectural or environmental sculpture. This, as has been noted, may be traced to its beginnings in small works, notably *Gothic Construction,* 1939, and has found its most monumental expression in the *Teodelapio,* 1962.

One of the first of the important new group of large black stabiles is *Black Widow,* dated 1959. This combines characteristics of the fantastic monster—in this case the mother of all poisonous spiders—with the environmental form. It is a lineal descendant of the 1940 *Black Beast.* From a body of interlocked, curving triangles emerge two enormous, attenuated, threatening legs supporting a small but sufficiently menacing head. At the other remove the body is an architectural-sculptural construction, and the legs form a graceful arch under which the spectator can pass.

The years 1963, and even more, 1964 and 1965, have seen the production of a tremendously varied group of great stabiles which may be roughly classified under this label. These include *Guillotine for Eight,* 1963, which with *Ghost,* hovering overhead, constituted the central focus of the Guggenheim Museum retrospective of Calder's works. Also included in that exhibition was *Bucephalus,* 1963, whose strong geometry of shapes still

Model for Jousting Knight, 1963

Octopus, 1964 and *Prickly Pear*, 1964

Polygon on Triangles (The Nun), 1964 (two views)

Black Widow, 1959—Collection
The Museum of Modern Art,
New York. Mrs. Simon
Guggenheim Fund.

Bucephalus, 1963

Slender Ribs, 1964

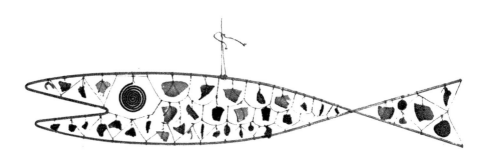

Fish, 1948-50

manages to retain the image of the charging warhorse. One of the most beautiful and graceful of the stabiles created during 1964 is *Slender Ribs,* which is now placed spectacularly at the edge of the ocean on the grounds of Louisiana Museum in Denmark. Several others, executed in the first months of 1965, were exhibited in the Calder exhibition at the Musée de l'Art Moderne in Paris. These included, together with many of those of earlier date, *Two Disks, Semaphore, Triangles, Heads and Queue, Triangles and Arches, Sabot, Wisdom Tooth (Dent de Sagesse),* and *Porc Qui Pic.* All of these are on a monumental scale and are listed to illustrate the tremendous artistic fecundity of the sculptor which seems to expand rather than diminish with age.

On November 15, 1965, the monumental stabile, *Guichet,* was installed before the Vivian Beaumont Theater at Lincoln Center in the city of New York. While this is beautifully placed on a great open plaza, it is again regrettable that the artist was not able to design a work specifically for the location. If he had, it would undoubtedly have been several times the scale of the present stabile, which is unfortunately dwarfed by the huge scale of the surrounding architecture. His most recent commissioned stabile, *La Grande Voile,* which is 40 feet high, was created to stand in front of a building by the architect I. M. Pei at Massachusetts Institute of Technology. Since Calder in this case has been able to relate the work in scale to its architectural surroundings, this is one of his most successful weddings of sculpture to architecture.

Conclusion

The great stabiles of the early sixties represent an obvious climax in the still-flourishing career of Alexander Calder. The progress which has been charted from circus drawings to the creation of an entire circus, from figurative and portrait wire sculptures to abstract wire constructions, from hand-powered to machine-powered to wind-powered mobiles, from hanging mobiles to standing mobiles to metal-plate stabiles on a monumental scale—all of this describes one of the most fertile and varied creative careers in the history of sculpture. However, even with all of this, the story is only partially told.

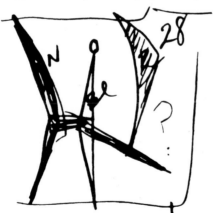

Calder began his career as a painter, draftsman and illustrator, and he has continued to draw and paint down to the present day. His illustrated books include *Animal Sketching,* 1926, *Fables of Aesop,* 1931, *Three Young Rats,* 1944, *The Rime of the Ancient Mariner,*

1946, and *Selected Fables of La Fontaine,* 1948. In recent years he has experimented extensively with lithography, and many of his designs have been translated into tapestries. His interest in painting has expanded enormously in the last few years, principally in the form of gouaches and water colors which range from pure abstractions reminiscent of those early attempts inspired by his visit to Mondrian's studio to fantastic, literally figurative works which provide a bridge between his fantastic metal-plate stabiles and a personal form of representational expression.

Calder has never ceased to make toys and gadgets for his own delectation and that of his numerous family and friends. The glass fish which ornament his home in Roxbury are chronological descendants but stylistic ancestors of the early broken glass and string mobiles. The *Sun* and the *Moon* of 1950 may be regarded as pure decorative fantasies. *The Only Only Bird* of 1952 transforms Medaglia d'Oro coffee cans into the gayest and most delightful of all feathered friends. On the other hand, such charming little beasts as *The Red Fox* and the *Little Black Dog,* of 1958, hover between the categories of toys and sculptures of serious intent, animals wonderfully and precisely characterized in a few twists of metal. *Rat,* 1952, is an even more ambiguous object, an abstract group of mobile units suspended on a tripod base which on examination transform themselves into one of the most repulsive little monsters ever created even by this artist's imagination.

The text of the present volume has concentrated on the sculptures, the mobiles and stabiles which are obviously Calder's greatest achievement. The photographs by Pedro Guerrero have expanded the story to illustrate the tremendous range of the artist's interests and activities, the totality of the environment which he has created and which is occupied by himself, his wife Louisa, and in various contexts by his children and grandchildren, and through which flows a constant, daily stream of friends, acquaintances, and casual visitors. The pace of a day at the Calders seems enough to exhaust the most hardy onlooker, but through it all the artist moves with benign calm, seeming ever-relaxed, and with all the time in the world to waste in the company of his innumerable friends (or even of strangers come to seek information). Yet in some miraculous manner, the creation of works of art, great and small, serious and occasionally facetious, goes on without interruption. Despite the great production, one can continually trace the growth of new ideas and **new forms which even in 1966 make him an** old master of modern art who is the most contemporary of living sculptors.

Utensils by Calder

The Only Only Bird, 1952

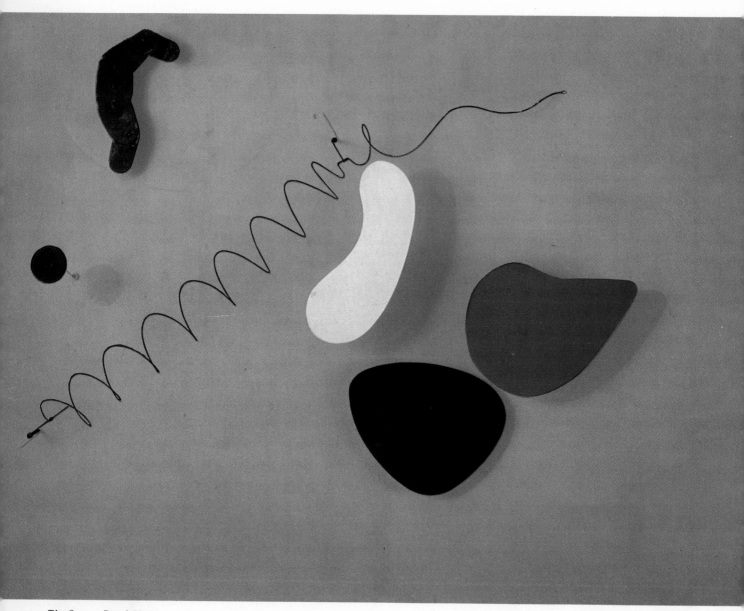

The Orange Panel, 1943

Four Elements, 1962, Moderna Museet, Stockholm.

Teodelapio, 1962, Spoleto.

Sabot, 1963; *Dent de Sagesse,* 1964—the view from Calder's studio, Saché

The kitchen, Roxbury

Southern Cross, 1963

Pots and Pans, 1964

Flags, 1964

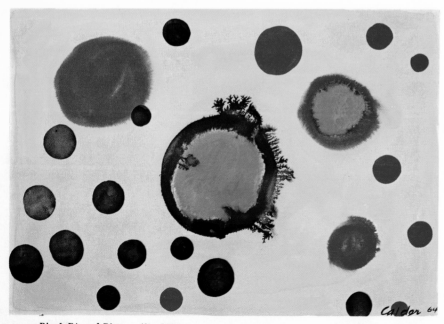

Black Ringed Blue et Alia, 1964

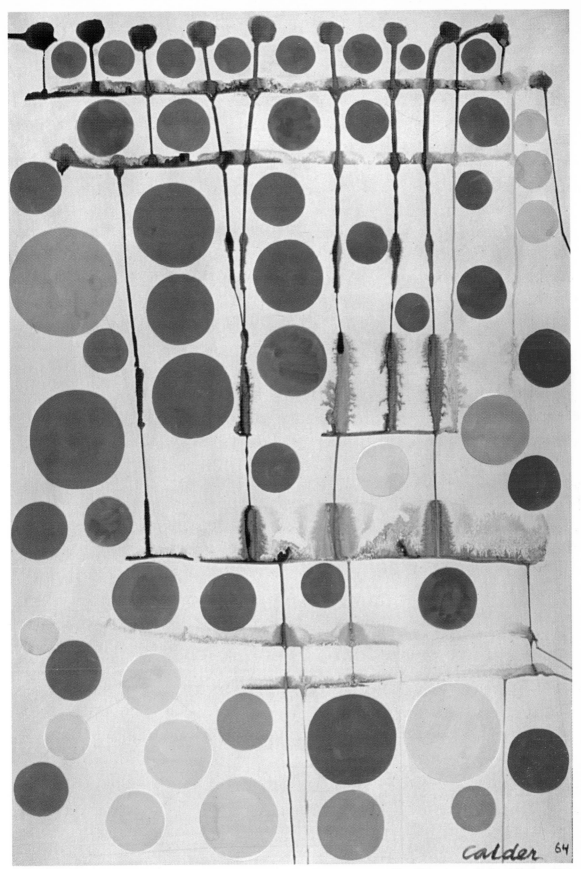

Five Blues Among Red and Yellow, 1964

Caduceus, 1962

Signs, 1962

Mouth, 1962

Mosquito, 1962

Whirligig, 1962

Black Head, 1962

Foundry at Tours, France, 1965

Chronology

WIRE SCULPTURE BY CALDER

to 1930

1898 Born in Philadelphia, July 22. His grandfather, Alexander Milne Calder, sculptor, born in Scotland, created the statue of William Penn on the dome of Philadelphia City Hall, as well as the equestrian statue of General Meade in Fairmount Park, Philadelphia. His father, A. Sterling Calder, was one of the leading American academic sculptors of his day. His mother was a painter. Calder thus grew up in a studio environment, but his own early inclinations were mechanical and he was drawn to engineering.

1915-1919 After study at Stevens Institute of Technology, he graduated with a degree in mechanical engineering.

1919-1923 Work as an engineer, and miscellaneous jobs and travel. In 1921 he began to take drawing lessons at night school in New York. In 1923, after travel to California and work in a logging camp in Washington State, he entered the Art Students' League in New York.

1923-1926 Study at the Art Students' League and work as an illustrator. Brief study with George Luks, Guy Pène Du Bois, and Boardman Robinson; intensive work with John Sloan. In 1924 he began doing illustrations for the *National Police Gazette*, and in 1925 he covered the circus for the *Gazette*. In 1926 he published a book on *Animal Sketching* and had his first exhibition of oil paintings at The Artist's Gallery, New York. The same year he made his first wood carving, entitled *Flattest Cat*.

1926-1927 In 1926 he went to Paris. There he met William Stanley Hayter and through him the sculptor, José de Creeft. He continued carving and in 1927 began making wire figures and animals as well as animated toys for his own amusement. The toys were exhibited in the *Salon des Humoristes,* in the spring of 1927. The wire figures and animals began to develop into a full-fledged circus. The circus performances which he gave in his room were visited by artists as well as by critics of the circus (who wrote enthusiastic accounts) and literary men, notably Jean Cocteau. The first completely realized wire figure sculpture was the *Josephine Baker*, 1926.

1927-1928 Return to New York during 1927. Toys were manufactured from his models. In his first one-man show of sculpture at the Weyhe Gallery, New York, February, 1928, he exhibited wire portraits and caricatures. He continued wood carving during this period. *Romulus and Remus*, a 10-foot-long wire sculpture, and *Spring*, another, 9 feet high, were exhibited at the *Independents* in New York. In November, 1928, he returned to Paris. There he met Miró who visited his circus performance. He also met Pascin through Kuniyoshi.

1929 January, exhibition largely of wire portraits and wood carvings at Galerie Billiet, Paris, with the catalogue preface by Pascin. Exhibition also during January, 1929, of *Spring* and *Romulus and Remus* at the *Indé-*pendants, Paris. In April, 1929, an exhibition of wire and wood sculptures was held at the Neumann-Nierendorf Gallery, Berlin. His first piece of jewelry was made in Berlin. Return to New York, June. Exhibition of wire and wood sculpture at the Fifty-sixth Street Galleries in December 1929. His first wire goldfish bowl was designed, in which the fish were moved by a hand crank.

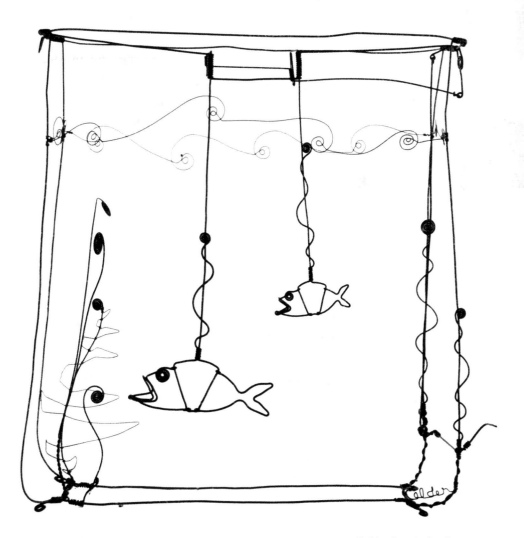

Fishbowl with Crank, 1929

Ben Hur

Ben Hur, 1931

Calder

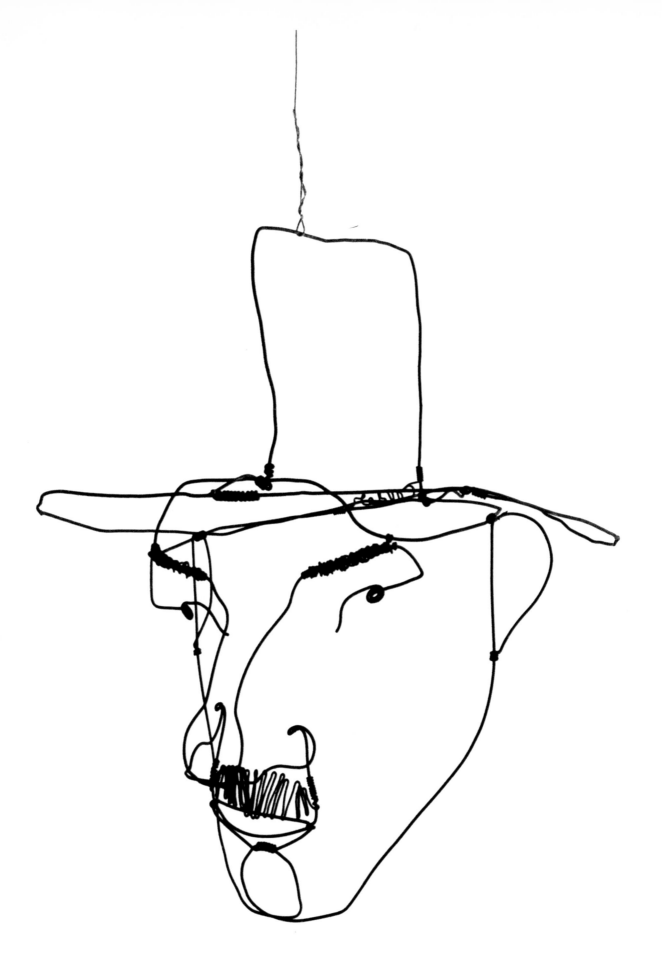

Léger, 1930

30-40

1930 Return to Paris, March, 1930. The fame of the circus had continued to grow. Performances were now visited by many artists, including Kiesler, Léger, Theo van Doesburg, and Mondrian. Calder was inspired by abstract painter William Einstein's enthusiastic description of Mondrian's significance to visit the latter's studio. As a result he experimented for the first time with abstract painting. He exhibited in the *XIe Salon de l' Araignée* and the *Salon des Surindépendants*, Paris. Return to New York the latter part of 1930. In a group exhibition at the Museum of Modern Art, *Paintings and Sculptures by Living Americans*. During 1930 he began to experiment with abstract wire sculptures, still static, introducing metal disks and other shapes painted in strong colors, blues, reds, and blacks. During 1929 and 1930 he continued exploring variants on crank-operated wire mobiles and other simple experiments in mechanical motion. These were still in the nature of toys, developing ideas originating in his circus groups.

1931 Married, January, 1931, to Louisa James. Return to Paris. He now began to meet with other leaders of abstract art, Theo van Doesburg, Jean Arp, and Jean Hélion, and joined the *Abstraction-Création* group of abstract artists. First exhibition of abstract wire constructions and wire portraits at Galerie Percier, Paris, with catalogue introduction by Fernand Léger. Illustrated book on the *Fables of Aesop*, Paris, 1931. Continued experiments with mechanical mobile sculptures, operated by hand or electric motors.

1932 First exhibition of hand and motor mobile constructions, Galerie Vignon, Paris. He also exhibited at the *Association Artistique '1940,'* Paris, and at the Julien Levy Gallery, New York. The constructions were named "mobiles" by Marcel Duchamp. Arp, seeing the Vignon exhibition, coined the phrase "stabiles" for non-moving constructions exhibited the previous year at the Galerie Percier. His growing friendship with Miró led to a visit to Miró in Spain in August, 1932.

1933 Calder, after Galerie Vignon exhibition, created the first free-floating or wind-operated mobiles. The very first wind mobile consisted of a version of the *Goldfish Bowl* in which two little fish moved freely on a pivot.

Steel Fish, 1934

160

This was made for his wife, Louisa, in the spring of 1933 and has long since disappeared. Visits and exhibition, in Madrid of the Circus, and in Barcelona, of drawings and constructions. Exhibition Galerie Pierre, Paris, with Miró, Arp, Pevsner, Hélion, and Kurt Seligmann. Growing influence of Miró in the move from geometric towards organic shapes. Exhibition Galerie Pierre Collé, Paris. Return to United States July 1933 and purchase of farm at Roxbury, Connecticut.

1934-1937   First of regular exhibitions with Pierre Matisse Gallery, New York. *Red Frame*, motorized panel mobile designed in Paris, lost or destroyed. The *White Frame*, 1934, largest motorized mobile to date, designed on return to U.S.A. *Steel Fish*, 1934, largest and most important standing mobile

to date. Settings for Martha Graham's *Panorama*, Bennington, Vermont, 1935. Birth of daughter Sandra in the spring of 1935. Settings for Eric Satie's *Socrate*, Wadsworth Atheneum, Hartford, Connecticut, 1936. "Plastic Interludes" for Martha Graham's *Four Movements*, New York, 1936. *Whale*, 1937, most monumental stabile to date. The *Mercury Fountain*, 1937, for the Spanish Pavilion of the Paris Exposition, most ambitious mobile project to date. Exhibition, Mayor Gallery, London, 1937.

1938-1939   October, exhibition *Trois Siècles d'Art aux États-Unis* at the Musée du Jeu de Paume. November, 1938, retrospective at George Walter Vincent Smith Art Museum, Springfield, Massachusetts. 1938, design of fountain, *Water Ballet*, for Consolidated Edison Company exhibit at 1939 New York World's Fair. The design was not carried out, due to mechanical problems. 1938, two models for large free-standing, motorized mobile for New York World's Fair. Project not carried out at the time. Daughter Mary born in 1939. First prize, Plexiglass Sculpture Competition, Museum of Modern Art, New York.

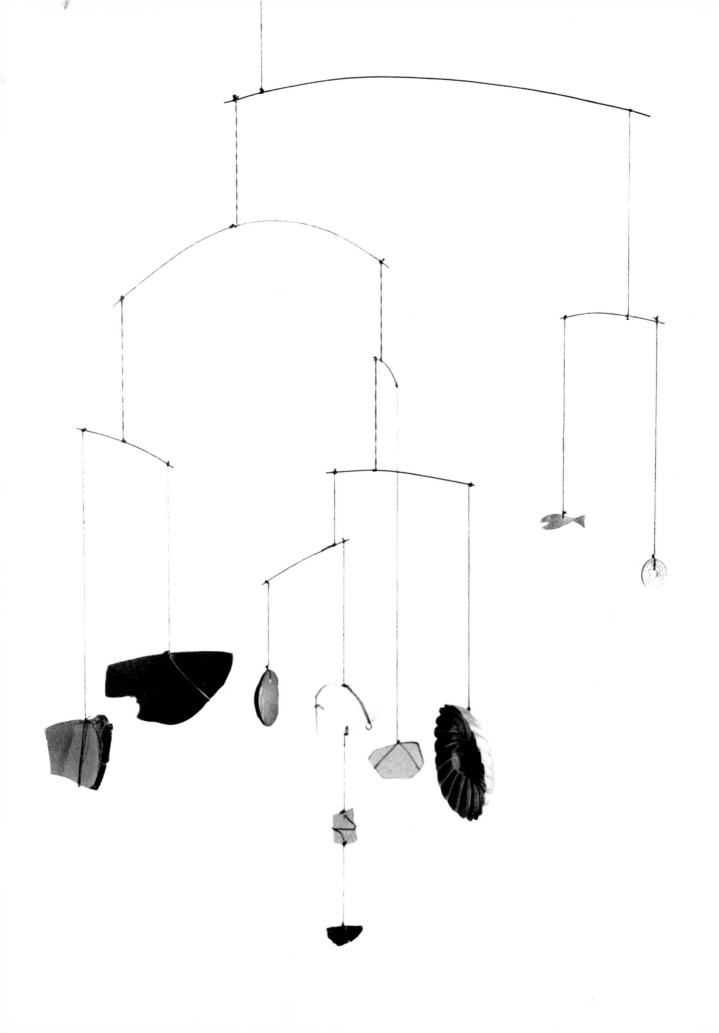

40-50

1940-1943   December, first exhibition of jewelry, Willard Gallery, New York. 1941, mobile for ballroom, Hotel Avila, Caracas, Venezuela. (This mobile now belongs to Aluminum Company of America, Pittsburgh.) Exhibition in the home of architect Wallace K. Harrison, Huntington, Long Island, 1941. 1943-1944, *Constellations,* stabiles and mobiles with organic shapes of painted or polished wood, joined by wire. November, 1943, major retrospective at the Museum of Modern Art, New York. Catalogue by James Johnson Sweeney, first major study of Calder.

1944-1948   Experiments with carved and modelled works, many cast in bronze, 1944. Began regular exhibitions at Buchholz (later Curt Valentin) Gallery, New York. Illustrated

Three Young Rats, edited by James Johnson Sweeney, 1944. Illustrated Robert Penn Warren's study of Coleridge, *The Rime of the Ancient Mariner,* 1945. 1945, return to Paris for visit. 1946, exhibition at Galerie Louis Carré, Paris. Introduction to catalogue by Jean-Paul Sartre. Major mobile for Terrace Plaza Hotel, Cincinnati, 1946. Illustrations for *The Fables of La Fontaine,* translated by Eunice Clark, 1946. 1947, exhibition with Léger, Stedelijk Museum, Amsterdam, and Kunsthalle, Berne. 1948, work on film with Herbert Matter, music by John Cage, narrative by Burgess Meredith. In 1948 he visited Brazil. Exhibition in Rio de Janeiro, Ministry of Education, and São Paulo, Museum of Art.

1949   Mobiles for "Symphonic Variations," ballet by Tatiana Leskova, music by César Franck, given in Rio de Janeiro. Exhibitions at Margaret Brown Gallery, Boston, and Museum of Fine Arts, Richmond, Virginia. 1949, largest mobile to date, *International Mobile,* 20 by 20 feet, designed for staircase, Philadelphia Museum of Art. (Not accepted by committee, later bought by The Museum of Fine Arts, Houston.)

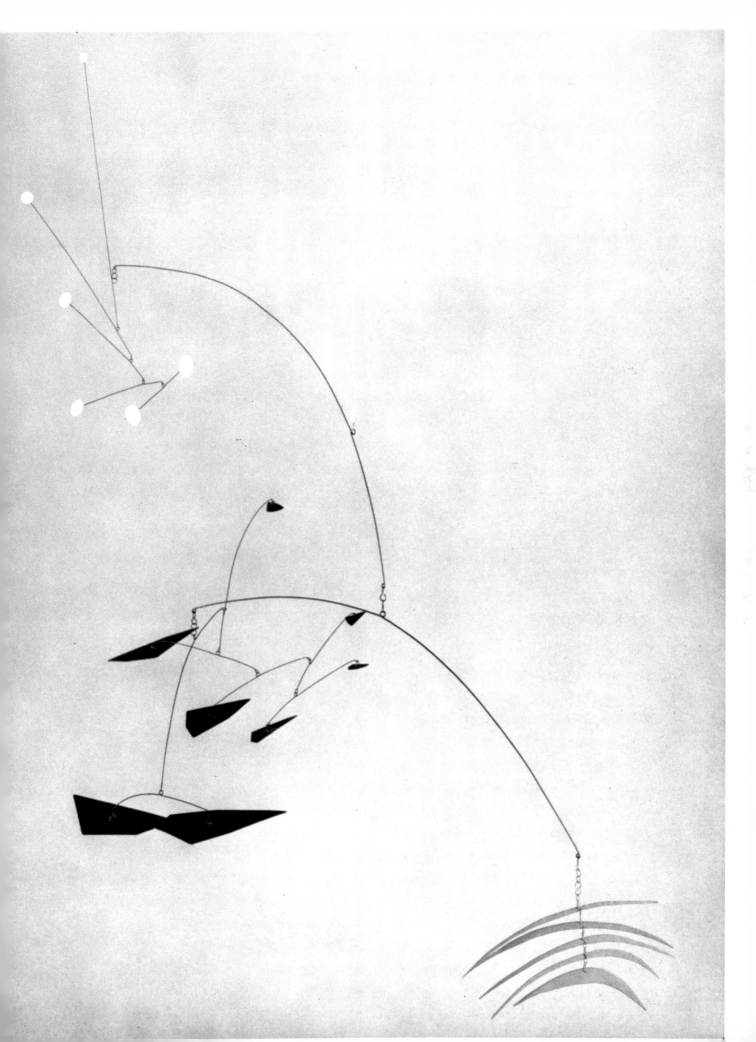

Bracelet

Three pins

Louisa Calder's combs

Seven necklaces for
Louisa Calder, 1940-50

50-60

1950 Began regular exhibition with Galerie Maeght, Paris. Chosen in *The New York Times*, November, 1950, as one of ten best illustrators of children's books of past 50 years. Major retrospective exhibition, Massachusetts Institute of Technology, Cambridge, December, 1950. Trips to Lascaux, London, Stockholm and Finland.

1951-1954 Acoustic ceiling for Aula Magna, University City, Caracas, Venezuela, 1952. First prize for sculpture, Venice Biennale, 1952. Acquired house and farm at Saché, Indre-et-Loire, France, 1953. 1953, exhibition with Naum Gabo; also, exhibition at Walker Art Center, Minneapolis. 1954, exhibition of gouaches, Galerie Cahiers d'Art. *Water Ballet* for General Motors Technological Center, Detroit, based on unrealized 1938 design for New York World's Fair. Started association with Perls Gallery, New York.

1955-1956 Visited India in 1955 and created 11 mobiles for Sarabhai Ahmedabad. Also 1955, exhibition at the Museo de Arte in Caracas. First of regular exhibitions at Perls Gallery, 1956. 1956, exhibition at Galleria dell'Obelisco, Rome, and exhibition of gouaches at Galerie Weill, Paris.

1957-1959 Monumental mobile (45-foot diameter) for Idlewild (Kennedy) Airport, 1957. *Whirling Ear*, motorized mobile for United States Pavilion, Brussels World's Fair; standing mobile for UNESCO, Paris, 1958. First prize, Carnegie International Exhibition, 1958. Exhibition, Galerie Maeght, Paris and Museu de Arte Moderno, Rio de Janeiro, 1959.

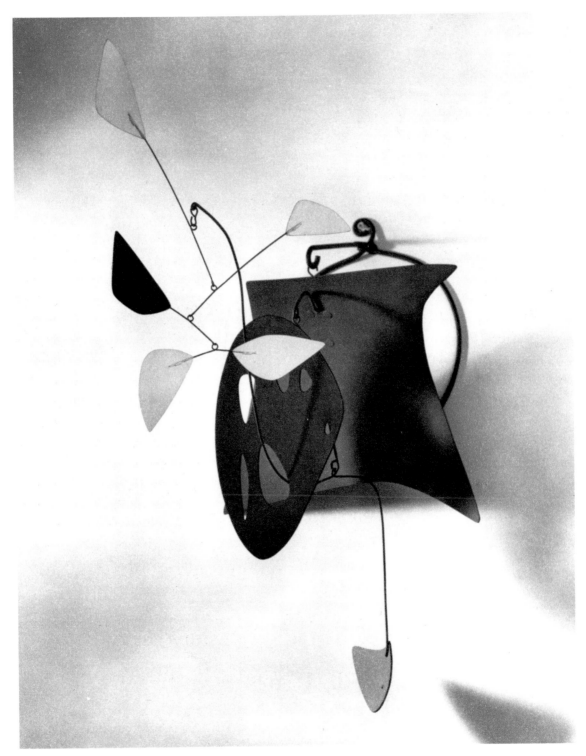

Black Sponge, 1958

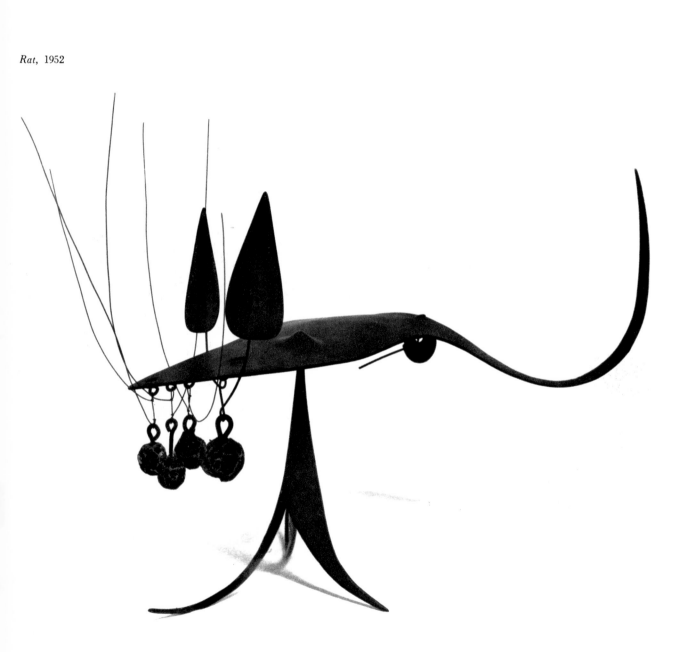

Rat, 1952

Little Black Dog, 1958

60—

1960-1961 Gold medal of Architectural League, New York, 1960. Medal, American Institute of Architects, 1961. Film of *Circus* with Vilardebo, 1961. Exhibition of gouaches and small mobiles in Caracas, 1961. Exhibition *Motion in Art* in Amsterdam, Stockholm, Copenhagen, 1961.

1962 Creative arts award for sculpture, Brandeis University, 1962. Retrospective exhibition, Tate Gallery, London, 1962. Retrospective exhibition, Musée des Beaux-Arts, Rennes, 1962, with catalogue preface by Jean Cassou. 1962, exhibition of gouaches 1948-62, Brook Street Gallery, London, *Teodelapio*, 1962, Spoleto, most monumental stabile to date, c. 60 feet high, designed for sculpture exhibition as an arched gateway to the city.

1963-1965 Exhibition of large stabiles, Galerie Maeght, Paris, 1963. 1963, exhibition, *Gouaches by Calder* at Galerie Alex Vömel, Düsseldorf. Five stabiles at *Docu-* *menta III* exhibition, Kassel, Germany, 1964. Exhibition of *Circus Drawings, Wire Sculpture and Toys*, Museum of Fine Arts in Houston, Texas, 1964. 1964, major fountain mobile, *Hello Girls!* for Los Angeles County Museum. In 1964-1965, the most comprehensive retrospective exhibition to date was organized by The Solomon R. Guggenheim Museum. The exhibition subsequently was shown in part at the Milwaukee Art Center, Washington University Art Gallery, St. Louis, Des Moines Art Center, and the National Gallery of Canada, Ottawa. The entire exhibition was shown with changes and additions at the Musée National d'Art Moderne, Paris, 1965.

1965—— November, 1965, major stabile, *Le Guichet*, for Lincoln Center in New York. 1965-1966, stabile *La Grande Voile*, 40 feet high, for Massachusetts Institute of Technology, Cambridge. Donated a large stabile, *Object in Five Planes*, to the United States Mission to the United Nations, February 1966.

Nazione, 1964

Funghi Neri, 1960;

Discontinuous, 1962

Untitled gouache, 1965

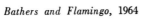

Bathers and Flamingo, 1964

Calder '64

Selected Bibliography

Illustrated by the artist

Animal Sketching. Pelham, New York, Bridgman Publishers, Inc., 1926.

Fables of Aesop. Paris, Harrison of Paris, 1931.

Three Young Rats and Other Rhymes. Edited with an introduction by James Johnson Sweeney, New York, Curt Valentin, 1944.

Samuel Taylor Coleridge, *The Rime of the Ancient Mariner.* With an essay by Robert Penn Warren, New York, Reynal and Hitchcock, 1946.

Jean de la Fontaine, *Selected Fables.* Translated by Eunice Clark, New York, Quadrangle Press, 1948.

A Bestiary. Edited by Richard Wilbur, New York, Pantheon Books, 1955.

"Alexander Calder's Circus." New York, *Art in America,* 1964, Facsimile lithographed portfolio.

Statements by the artist

Abstraction-Création, Art Non Figaratif. 1:6, 1932. Translated in *Art of This Century,* Ed. Peggy Guggenheim, New York, 1942.

Berkshire Museum, Pittsfield, Massachusetts, *Modern Painting and Sculpture,* August, 1933. Exhibition catalogue.

The Painter's Object. Ed. Myfanwy Evans, London, 1937.

Addison Gallery of American Art, Andover, Massachusetts, *Mobiles by Calder.* June, 1943. Exhibition catalogue.

The Tiger's Eye. no. 4:74, June 1948.

"What Abstract Art Means to Me," *Museum of Modern Art Bulletin,* New York 18 no. 3:8, Spring 1951.

Alvard, Julien and Gindertael, R. V. eds., *Témoignages pour l'art abstrait 1952,* Paris, Èditions "Art d'aujourd 'hui," 1952.

Selden Rodman, *Conversations with Artists,* New York, 1957.

George W. Staempfli, "Interview with Calder," *Quadrum,* no. 6, 1959.

Katherine Kuh, *The Artist's Voice: Talks with Seventeen Artists,* New York, 1962.

Selected Books

Museum of Modern Art, New York, *Cubism and Abstract Art.* New York, 1936.

Valentiner, W., *Origins of Modern Sculpture,* New York, Wittenborn, 1946.

Yale University Art Gallery, *Collection of the Société Anonyme: Museum of Modern Art, 1920,* New Haven, Connecticut, 1950.

Ritchie, Andrew, *Sculpture of the Twentieth Century,* Museum of Modern Art, New York, 1952.

Seuphor, Michel, *La Sculpture de ce Siècle,* Neuchatel, Editions du Griffon, 1959.

Giedion-Welcker, Carola, *Contemporary Sculpture,* New York, Wittenborn, 1960.

Trier, Edward, *Form and Space,* New York, Praeger, 1961.

Arnason, H. Harvard, *Modern Sculpture from the Joseph H. Hirshhorn Collection,* The Solomon R. Guggenheim Foundation, New York, 1962.

Selected Periodicals

Jakovski, Anatole, "Alexander Calder," *Cahiers d'Art,* 3, no. 5-6, 1933.

Sweeney, James Johnson, "Alexander Calder," *Axis,* no. 3, July 1935.

Sweeney, James Johnson, "Alexander Calder: movement as a plastic element," *Architectural Forum,* 70, Feb. 1939.

Sweeney, James Johnson, "The Position of Alexander Calder," *Magazine of Art,* 37, May 1944.

Sartre, Jean-Paul, "Des Mobiles," *Style en France,* no. 5, April 15, 1947, from Carré catalogue 1946.

Sartre, Jean-Paul, "Existentialist on mobilist: Calder's newest works judged by France's newest philosopher," *Art News* 46, no. 10, Dec. 1947.

Sartre, Jean-Paul, "Calder," *Art Présent,* Paris, no. 3, 1947.

Janis, Harriet, "Mobiles," *Arts & Architecture* 65, no. 2, Feb. 1948.

Masson, André, "L'Atelier de Calder," *Cahiers d'Art* 24, no. 2, 1949.

"Calder," *Derrière Le Miroir,* no. 31, July 1950.

Clapp, Talcott, "Calder," *Art d'Aujourd'hui,* no. 11, June 1950.

Schiller, Ronald "Calder" *Portfolio, the Annual of the Graphic Arts,* Cincinnati, The Zebra Press, New York, Duell, Sloane and Pearce, 1951.

Schmidt, Georg, "Alexander Calder's 'Mobiles,'" *Du,* Zürich, vol. 13, December 1953.

Derrière le Miroir, Paris, nos. 69-70, October-November 1954. Issue devoted to Calder, Contains Henri Pichette, "Poème offert à Alexander Calder et à Louisa;" Frank Elgar, "Calder;" checklist of exhibition, Galerie Maeght, Paris, October-November 1954.

Brugière, P. G., "L'objet-mobile de Calder," *Cahiers d'Art*, Paris, vol. 29, no. 2, 1954.

Derrière le Miroir, Paris no. 113, 1959. Issue devoted to Calder, Contains Jean Davidson, "Le luron aux protège-genoux;" Georges Salles, "Stabiles;" checklist of exhibition Galerie Maeght, Paris, March-April 1959.

Gasser, Helmi, "Alexander Calder," *Werk*, Zürich, vol. 46, no. 12, December 1959.

Restany, Pierre, "L'autre Calder," *Art International*, Zürich, vol. 3, nos. 5-6 1959.

Rickey, George, "Calder in London," *Arts*, New York, vol. 36, no. 10, September 1962.

Rickey, George, "The Morphology of Movement," *College Art Journal*, Summer 1963.

Sweeney, James Johnson, "Alexander Calder: Work and Play," *Art in America*, New York, vol. 51, no. 4, August 1963.

Derrière le Miroir, Paris, no. 141, November 1963. Issue devoted to Calder. Contains James Jones, "L'ombre de l'avenir;" Michel Ragon, "Qu'est-ce qu'un Calder?"; color lithographs by Calder.

Gray, Cleve, "Calder's Circus, *Art in America*, New York, vol. 52, no. 5, October 1964.

Gruppy, Nicholas, "Alexander Calder," *Atlantic Monthly*, December 1964.

Lemon, Richard, "The Soaring Art of Alexander Calder," *Saturday Evening Post*, February 27, 1965.

"Mobile Maker's Giddy Whirl," *Life*, March 5, 1965.

Anderson, Wayne V., "Calder at the Guggenheim," *Art Forum* Vol. III, no. 6, 1965.

Selected Exhibition Catalogues

Galerie, Billiet, Paris, Jan. 25-Feb. 7, 1929; preface by Pascin.

Galerie Percier, Paris. *Alexander Calder*, April 27-May 9, 1931; foreword by Fernand Léger.

Arts Club, Chicago, *Mobiles by Alexander Calder*, Feb 1-26; 1935; preface by J. J. Sweeney.

Museum of Modern Art, New York, *Fantastic Art, Dada, Surrealism*, 1936; Ed. by Alfred H. Barr, Jr.

George Walter Vincent Museum, Springfield, Massachusetts, *Calder Mobiles*, Nov 8-27, 1938; preface by J. J. Sweeney.

Art of this Century, New York, *Art of this Century, 1910-1942*; ed. by Peggy Guggenheim.

The Cincinnati Modern Art Society, Cincinnati, *Paintings by Paul Klee and Mobiles and Stabiles by Alexander Calder*, April 7-May 3, 1942.

Museum of Modern Art, New York, *Alexander Calder*, Sept. 29-Jan. 16, 1943; by J. J. Sweeney, revised edition 1951.

Louis Carré Galerie, Paris, *Alexander Calder; Mobiles, Stabiles, Constellations*, Oct. 25-Nov. 16, 1946; essay by Jean-Paul Sartre.

Ministório da Educacao e Saude, Rio de Janeiro, *Alexander Calder*, September 1948; text by Sartre.

Galerie Blanche, Stockholm, *Alexander Calder: Mobiles et Stabiles*, December 1950; foreword by Eric Grate; text in Swedish.

Kunsthalle, Basel, *Calder*, 1957; introduction by Arnold Rüdlinger.

Stedelijk Museum, Amsterdam, *Alexander Calder*, 1951; contains Georges Salles "Stabiles," W. Sandberg, "Calder und die mobiles."

Palais des Beaux-Arts, Brussels, *Calder*, April 3-May 1, 1960; text by Georges Salles.

Kunstgewerbemuseum, Zürich, *Kinetische Kunst, Alexander Calder, Mobiles und Stabiles aus den letzten Jahren*, May-June 1960; Introduction by Hans Fischli and Willi Rotzler.

The Arts Council of Great Britain, London, *Alexander Calder*, July 4-August 12, 1962; introduction by James Johnson Sweeney.

Documenta III, Kassel, *Malerei und Skulptur*, June 27-October, 1964, vol. 1.

The Solomon R. Guggenheim Museum, New York, *Alexander Calder*, November 5-January 31, 1965; introduction by Thomas M. Messer.

The Museum of Fine Arts, Houston, Texas, *Alexander Calder*, November 24–December 13, 1964; introduction by James Johnson Sweeney.

Musée National D'Art Moderne, Paris, *Calder*, July-October 1965.

Regular exhibitions of Calder's works have been held at the Buchholz, Curt Valentin, Pierre Matisse and Perls Galleries in New York and the Galerie Maeght in Paris.

Note: For a more comprehensive bibliography until 1951, see James Johnson Sweeney, *Alexander Calder*, New York, Museum of Modern Art, 1951. For works published after this date, consult the catalogue of the Calder exhibition at The Solomon R. Guggenheim Museum, New York, 1964.

Chronology of Works

Collection the artist unless otherwise noted.

187

188

Index

Works of art and page references to illustrations are shown in italic.